Try Not to Think of an Orange

Try not to Think of an Orange

High Profile Tactics for Super Salespeople

John R. Downes

Writers Club Press
San Jose New York Lincoln Shanghai

Try not to Think of an Orange
High Profile Tactics for Super Salespeople

Writers Club Press
an imprint of iUniverse.com, Inc.

For information address:
iUniverse.com, Inc.
5220 S 16th, Ste. 200
Lincoln, NE 68512
www.iuniverse.com

ISBN: 0-595-14090-4

Printed in the United States of America

FOR SUSAN
She bears witness
to all these precepts.

Strange! all this difference should be
'Twixt Tweedledum and Tweedledee.
JOHN BYROM

Like, but oh! how different!
WORDSWORTH

Man's capacities have never been measured.
THOREAU

Introduction

What is it about the achievers in this world that causes them to be successful, while the rest simply tiptoe in place and accept the status quo? If you're constantly pressing the envelope, you know how special you are. Being unique and a top performer requires conscious, super effort and a zeal to stand in the spotlight. Your name on the marquee is one of the rewards.

Recognition, praise, and riches belong to those who dare to make life substantially greater…and not just for themselves. History books showcase achievers who stood out, were unique, and had the ability and guts to change their lives and environments. Each was solely responsible for his or her own success.

This book about creative persuasion reveals and explains how to use specific techniques…high profile tactics, that will enrich your individuality and performance even more, and will provide you with new weapons for persuasion-ability. Herein lies a philosophy that encourages a person you choose to persuade to reach out for a product or service or point of view in much the same way a kitten reaches out for a ball of yarn. The prospect's reaching out is what causes him to know he wants it and results in persuasion.

The high profile tactics you'll add to your repertoire are: The Fifth W, Matching Up, Pulling the String, Guts to Fail, Asking for a Turndown, Ray Gun, Lofty Platitudes, Theater of the Mind, Turn Into Columbo, Non-Negotiable Factors, Trip to Europe Questions, FBI Interrogation School Questions, Stacking the Bricks, Cliffhangers, Plastic Bucket, Yo-yo Effect, Mystifying Statements, Carrots, and Star Quality. They're adaptable to any selling situation…and fun to read about, learn, and put into practice.

Throughout this book, you'll witness the success of a character named Jimmy Dover, who is an expert practitioner of these high profile sales tactics. He's not a philosopher; he's an achiever. At times he's humble and low-key; occasionally thoughtful and reflective; sometimes vulnerable; but always original, stimulating, upbeat, and productive. In each situation, his personality shifts slightly. He reshapes himself to fit the circumstance, engages people at their own levels of understanding, and puts them in touch with their already present inclinations to desire something. He interacts with other characters: Mr. Big, Billy Bologne, Steve Stroker, Mike Mallis, Short Little Round Man, Mrs. Guardian, Mr. Principal, Harold and Helen Homesteader, Barry Berry, Venus Cauldron, Gloria Goodshape, Mr. Wormwood and others. Jimmy Dover climbs inside their brains and probes easily with a boyish charm, naivete and puzzling innocence that's purposeful, disarming, and effective.

He makes it look easy. But it's not. It's extremely difficult. While most people can swing a tennis racket, few can return a Pete Sampras serve. Achievers are the bright lights…constantly pressing the envelope. The status quo bores them. Pedestals attract. Constant improvement keeps them masters of their universe.

John R. Downes

Contents

Chapter One

The Fifth "W"

The Orange

For the next twenty minutes, try not to think of an orange.

That challenge will be difficult to accomplish, if not impossible, as it's composed of a persuasive ingredient that's like the changing tide. One cannot wrap his arms around it, nor know absolutely how or why it exists. Similar to hypnosis, it remains suspended in one's mind until it's triggered by a phrase.

To prove it, throughout this book you'll come across the simple question..."What are you thinking of?" And like a light bulb turning on, so will that big, juicy, round fruit envelop and capture your brain. To some readers, it's size will resemble a pumpkin. In Technicolor yet.

Similarly, when you embrace the precepts set out in this book and establish, as a result, the persona for yourself that will ensue from your mastery of them, your sales prospects won't be able to get you out of their minds either...as hard as they may try. But, why should they? They'll yearn to think about you.

Even though many communications contain the who, what, where and when, most lack the Fifth W, which causes them to stand out and be one-of-a-kind...the Wow. Outstanding impact requires it. Try to remember one television commercial from last night? Next, recall one ad you saw in yesterday's newspaper. Now, visualize a billboard you've seen recently. Is your mind cluttered with mixed images, or does it resemble the landscape of the moon? Bring to mind a radio commercial you've listened to within the past twenty-four hours. And the product or service it ballyhooed. Are you reading slower?

Billions of dollars are spent each year for advertising. Many are wasted on hackneyed, unmemorable, self-serving, lofty platitudes and hyperbole. Advertising imitates itself and is simply a clone of the competition's...with rare exceptions, of course, like: "You can take Salem out of the country, but...". Or "The pause that...". How about, "You're in good hands with...". Or, "When you care enough to send...". And, "Does she or doesn't...". Exceptions aside, me-tooism pervades. When consumers are surveyed, their minds turn into a vacuum. Remembering is based on just three reasons:

1. You need the product or service right now.
2. You already use the product or service.
3. The ad contains the Fifth W.

Try to recall one of the floats in the Rose Bowl Parade. A garbage truck entry is more memorable than one of the prize floats, because it's uniquely different from the rest. Most of us want our work to stand out and be recognized. We strive to succeed and make meaningful contributions to our professions. The Fifth W is vital.

What are you thinking of?

The Fifth W need not be lengthy. It can be a brief moment, such as the few seconds a great play in a sporting event requires. Many have seen news films of Babe Ruth pointing to center field to indicate where he intended to hit a home run followed by his hitting a home run to that spot...truly a memorable moment that took less than thirty seconds. Nobody can recall, though, what he did during the remainder of that game. Or for the rest of the season, for that matter. Radio commercials are thirty or sixty seconds in length, but five seconds may be more than enough to cause the desired impact. Consider the following:

* * *

Short Short Commercial

"Think of a large stainless steel vat...a mile wide, a mile long, and a mile deep filled with delicious Doverland Milk. Now, think of the poor cow!"

The Fifth W does not need to be a mere moment. It can reside in every part of something and be a combination of dazzling ingredients, each by themselves having memorability and Wow. The cumulative effect creates an overwhelming compulsion to obtain it. Desire engulfs the beholder. Putting it out of one's mind is not an option. The following situation could have been an ordinary event in a work day of Mr. Gray, but Jimmy Dover knows the importance of stirring The Fifth W into the recipe that includes his product, company name, sales presentation, and himself.

*   *   *

Raps Wraps Are Really Wonderful

It resembled a government office, but it wasn't. A gray desk, gray cabinet, and gray tables cluttered the gray office of Mr. Gray, the senior school supply buyer for the national variety store chain headquartered in New York City. It was easy to know that Mr. Gray was the senior school supply buyer, because the door to his office held a gray sign that read, "Mr. Gray...Senior School Supply Buyer." Other clues were various school supply items stacked on shelves and spilling off tables and chairs of his office.

Six months earlier, Jimmy Dover had organized a company to manufacture subject folders. With two horizontal pockets, they were used by students to hold their notes. A popular slang expression for students at that time was "rap." When kids talked to each other, they "rapped." When kids put their school work inside the folders, they "wrapped" their notes. Jimmy thus coined the name Rap Wrap for the product.

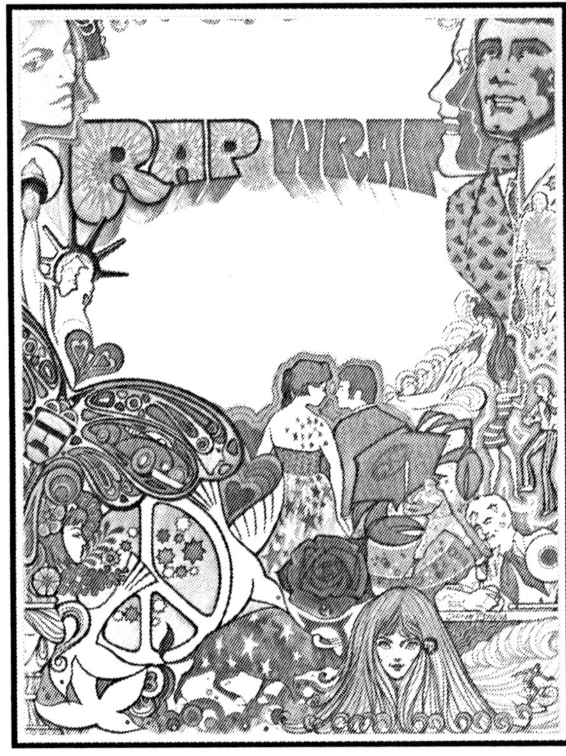

He followed that up less than one year later with Doodlers, a black and white folder that had special appeal to elementary school age children, because they could color it in themselves; although it proved to be a big hit with high school and college students, too.

Some huge companies were well established in the folder business. Before Rap Wraps could obtain big-time distribution, Jimmy recognized the challenge of attracting the favor of top executives employed by the major chains. The Fifth W was vital in all aspects. Besides the product's name, though, Jimmy knew the graphics must be aimed at its users...the students, instead of its buyers...the moms and dads. He perceived that young people were interested in five basic themes that year: zodiac, American flag, religion, peace, and heritage; so he created artwork and photography to convey those five subjects as cover designs; then created a marketing tool, the acronym ZARPH, which utilized the first initial of each, and challenged distributors throughout America to observe the absence of ZARPH from competing companies, whose lackluster designs fit into two broad categories...floral patterns and plain colors. Jimmy named his company Lettuce...after the vegetable. He reasoned that if the Beatles recording company could be Apple, why couldn't his be Lettuce? For the logo, he chose a banana hanging by a frayed string.

Jimmy sat in Mr. Gray's office, at the pinnacle of the general merchandising business. Anyone could make an appointment with Mr. Gray, but selling him a new product was a different matter, as his reputation in the trade was a very hard sell. Jimmy knew that success with him would influence distribution at similar-sized and smaller chains throughout the United States, as they liked to follow the leader.

"For decades, Mr. Gray," said Jimmy, "the retail school supply business has been a contest every year between the big chains to see who could lose the most money on 500 count notebook paper. It's profitable for the manufacturers, but not for the retailers. Why? Because the merchandising is all aimed at the penny pinchers, mom and dad...the buyers, instead of the kids themselves...the users. But the kids know how to get what they want, Mr. Gray, and if the right graphics are used with the product, they'll pressure their parents to get it for them. Look at the toy companies. And the cereal companies. Do they advertise on the six o'clock news because that's what mom and dad watch? Of course not! They advertise on the Saturday morning cartoon shows for the kiddies...and rock stations and tv programs catering to the high schoolers for the teen demographics. Do parents watch those? Of course not! But who demands the products? The kids!"

Mr. Gray listened without expression as Jimmy continued.

"Up until now," said Jimmy, "the so-called choice in the school supply category has been between a red folder or a white folder. In the next couple of minutes, I'll show you how we're changing all that."

Jimmy appeared optimistic as he spoke, but he made no move to show his samples yet.

"It already has changed, Mr. Dover," interrupted Mr. Gray. "Several companies this year are introducing graphics into their lines to appeal to kids. Let me show you."

Mr. Gray reached down to the floor for a small stack of folders and fanned them out on his desk. In pastel colors, one design was a rainbow. Another was a field of tulips. A third was a photograph of a young girl standing in a pond throwing rose petals in the air.

Jimmy glanced at them and without hesitation said, "Mr. Gray, I'd like to ask you to do me a little favor. Of course, we've just met, and you may feel it's presumptuous of me. So, I'd like to get your permission first to ask the favor."

"You have it."

"I'd like to ask that you close your eyes for a moment."

Mr. Gray complied.

"I want you to imagine yourself as a sophomore in high school," said Jimmy. "Will you do that?"

"Are Sloppy Joes on the menu?"

"Go ahead and think about one of the designs you just showed me. Have you got one in mind?"

"Resembles Holland."

"It makes no difference which one, but let me ask you this, Mr. Gray. Thinking of yourself as a sophomore high school boy, would you buy it?"

"No?"

"Of course you wouldn't. It's too feminine. Boys won't buy it. That's half the market right there...boys! Why not insist, with your limited shelf space, on the product line that appeals to girls and boys at the same time. Open your eyes and I'll show you."

Twenty minutes later Mr. Gray said, "You've just made your first sale to my company." Then he carefully stacked the competitors' folders atop his desk, lifted them over the wastebasket, and dropped them in.

*   *   *

Try to imagine the presentations that Mr. Gray usually heard...mundane, ordinary, forgettable...with as much charisma as on old piece of bubble gum. Putting The Fifth W to work (with another high profile tactic...Theater of the Mind, which we'll read about in chapter five), Jimmy positioned the strength of his product against the weakness of all the competitors', and he caused Mr. Gray to identify with the ultimate purchasers...high school boys. "Where's the Zarph?" became the battle cry.

Another effective approach that's related to The Fifth W is the Arresting Trademark. Aren't two functions of a trademark to 1). identify a company or service or product and 2). cause it to stand out and be memorable? Some are effective, some aren't. Entertainers have trademarks. Consider: Jay Leno's pompadour and long chin; Bill Gates glasses; Regis Philbin's "Is that your final answer?"; Larry King's sleeve garters; Tiger Wood's pumping fist and red shirt. What's your trademark? Jimmy Dover's Rap Wraps could have been named Northwest Folders or some other bland name and remained anonymous.

What are you thinking of?

*   *   *

The Head of Lettuce Strikes Again

The following week, Jimmy Dover was a guest speaker at a downtown civic club. Questions followed his talk on marketing and advertising.

"Why is the name of your company Lettuce, but your trademark a banana?"

"Would you mind if I answered your question with a question?" replied Jimmy.

"Of course not," said the questioner.

"What company do you work with?"

"Acme Concrete Company."

"Does your company have a trademark or logo that it uses on its letterhead and in its advertising?"

"Of course."

"Does anyone ever ask you about it?"

"No."

"Everybody asks about my banana."

Something has to be noticed before anything occurs. The Fifth W and Arresting Trademarks are necessities for being memorable. Grabbing consumers by their eyeballs are their functions. Suppose you're standing in a long line. Everyone is waiting to apply for one job opening. And you know that the employer will make his selection by simply standing in front of each person, saying nothing, requiring no information other than a first impression. What can you do to improve the odds for your selection?

Tough, isn't it?

That's what retail businesses do, you know. They cluster together downtown, in malls, strip centers, along arterials, begging shoppers to notice them. One storefront after another cries out for attention with diverse signs and colors, exterior decorations, window displays, et al. Some succeed. Some don't. What's the difference between success and failure?

The Fifth W.

Retail stores compete for attention the same way job applicants do. Suppose one of the applicants is short, red-haired, and freckled. Further suppose that the others are all tall, good looking, and wearing blue blazers and shined shoes. Would that enhance or diminish the freckle-faced applicant's chances for being noticed? What if someone whispered to the employer before the inspection to try not to notice the freckle-faced redhead? Would he? Could he? By the way, what are you thinking of?

Another perspective. Suppose that Steve Martin were standing in that line. Or Jonathan Winters. Or Carol Burnett. Or Snoopy. Or Colin Powell. Or Eddie Murphy. What would they do to create attention without saying anything?

Challenging, isn't it? Nobody said it was easy. If it were, this world would be way too competitive. Besides, The Fifth W is necessary only for those who strive to be successful. How many successful people do you know personally? Jimmy Dover's success has a lot to do with his ability to use an Arresting Trademark and The Fifth W in every facet of his presentation.

In the following situation, Jimmy starts out as a complete stranger, yet everyone he encounters advances him toward his goal.

*　　　　*　　　　*

No Appointment

Jimmy Dover emerged from the taxicab and walked into the large headquarters building of the regional grocery chain in Chicago. More than sixty salespeople waited in the spacious reception room to see one of the many buyers. They stood in small groups talking quietly or sat quietly on the various couches and chairs. Jimmy approached the receptionist.

"My name is Jimmy Dover. Could you please tell me the name of the school supply buyer?"

"What kind of school supplies?"

"Rap Wrap subject folders. Kids use them to keep their notes in."

"That's Mr. Principal. Did you say Rap Wraps?"

"Yes."

"What's the name of your company, Mr. Dover?"

"Lettuce"

"What?"

"Lettuce."

"Like the vegetable?"

"That's right. Here's my card. I guess Mr. Principal is the man I came to see."

"Do you have an appointment?" She gazed at Jimmy's card.

"No."

"You must have an appointment to see him. Is this really your card?"

"I'm the Head of Lettuce all the way from the West Coast."

"That won't help. Most of these people are from out of town. They phoned or sent a fax requesting an appointment with one of the buyers for today. I'm sorry."

Jimmy looked distraught. "What about Mr. Principal's secretary?"

"I'll ring her office." The receptionist dialed the phone. "Mrs. Guardian? There's a Mr. Dover out here selling Rap Wraps. He's the Head of Lettuce. He wants an appointment with Mr. Principal. What? Yes. Lettuce. Like the vegetable. Yes. L-E-T-T-U-C-E. Yes. He's here right now.

He doesn't have an appointment. Yes. He's the Head of Lettuce. Yes. Lettuce. That's right. And he's selling Rap Wraps. Rap Wraps! What? Oh. R-A-P-W-R-A-P. Thank you."

The receptionist replaced the receiver and looked up at Jimmy. "I believe Mrs. Guardian will be right with you. May I keep your card?"

"Sure."

"What does the banana have to do with it?"

"Quite a bit. See that string? It's frayed. The banana is hanging from the top of the card by that string. Everybody tells me I've got a very heavy banana." Jimmy's voice had the tone of a coroner.

"That's cute. That's really cute," exclaimed the receptionist in a voice louder than she'd planned.

"Thank you. You're very kind."

She laughed out loud and held her hand to her mouth. At that moment a well-groomed, attractive woman approached from a long hallway.

"Are you the Head of Lettuce?" she asked.

"Yes. Mrs. Guardian?"

"Yes. Jimmy Dover?"

"Yes."

Her careful demeanor loosened, and she broke out into a broad grin. "It's nice to meet you, Mr. Dover. Will you follow me please? You've piqued my boss's curiosity."

After walking through a hallway labyrinth, they entered Mr. Principal's office.

"Mr. Principal," she said, "this is Jimmy Dover."

"So you're the Head of Lettuce." Mr. Principal's voice boomed through the large room. "Sit down."

Mrs. Guardian departed and closed the door.

"I don't quite know what's come over me," said Mr. Principal. "I broke a couple of company rules just now by inviting you in here without an appointment." Jimmy remained silent.

"May I see your business card, Jimmy?"

Jimmy reached into his right-hand jacket pocket. No card. He reached into his left-hand jacket pocket. No card there either. "I believe I'm fresh out. No, wait a minute. I know." He pulled out his wallet and searched through it. "I usually keep one in here. Nope. Gone."

Mr. Principal watched him expectantly.

"Oh wait!" exclaimed Jimmy. "Here…no…yes…here's one. It got stuck behind my Australian two dollar bill. It's a little dog-eared. Hope that's okay." Jimmy handed it to him.

Mr. Principal grinned. "You know, Jimmy, when my secretary informed me that the Head of Lettuce was in the lobby to sell me some Rap Wraps, I just had to meet you. What are Rap Wraps?"

Jimmy wrote a huge order that day. He made an impact on everybody he talked to. The Fifth W was clearly at work. That company's reception room was filled with other salespeople who were well dressed, professional, polite, prepared and invisible; but nothing motivated any of the buyers to break rules to meet any of them out of turn or without an appointment. Mr. Principal had a compulsion to meet Jimmy Dover.

* * *

Consider a comedian at the start of his act. His first few seconds are critical. He must build instantaneous rapport with the audience. A good introduction certainly helps, but still, he's on his own. Have you ever watched a first-time performer on the Tonight Show? Viewers ask themselves, "Who's that guy?" It's tougher for him to succeed than the established entertainer, whose reputation precedes him. Comedian Jim Carrey needs only to walk on stage, and the audience laughs uproariously. Did that occur the first time he'd appeared? Of course not. Steve Martin can simply utter his exaggerated "Well, excuuuuse meeee," and the audience howls.

Jimmy Dover had no guarantee he'd succeed with Mr. Principal. The receptionist could have been unresponsive, as could have been Mrs.

Guardian. What is guaranteed is that had Jimmy acted like everyone else, he certainly would not have seen Mr. Principal that day. Exceptions are made for those who practice high profile sales tactics.

Some people can fold laundry irresistibly…think of Red Skelton. How about Woody Allen? Or your neighbor's little girl? Or your history teacher? There are thousands of ways to be average. It takes preparation and adherence to certain principles to stand out and scream Wow.

What are you thinking of?

* * *

Wormwood's Big Event

Mr. Wormwood considered himself a trendsetter. He'd stocked up heavily on smile buttons just before the fad faded. After that…pet rocks. He was also well-stocked for the next hula hoop craze, since he still had several hundred remaining from the last one. His office was done in knotty pine. Several bowling trophies sat atop his desk near a photograph of him holding a trout.

"Tell me, Mr. Dover, does your company have other products besides Rap Wraps," he asked.

"One big advantage," replied Jimmy, "about having a product that's made of paper is the flexibility of being able to move into other product categories besides school supplies. We're almost ready to launch a new product. I wouldn't mind giving you a sneak preview if you'd share your opinion with me."

"What is it?"

Jimmy lifted his sample case onto his lap and opened the lid slightly…then closed it, and placed it at the foot of his chair.

"No. Wait. Let me say something about it first," he said.

Wormwood's anticipatory look turned to disappointment. His hand tightened on the edge of his desk as he gazed at the sample case.

Jimmy continued. "You know how when shoppers are waiting at the checkout stand in the supermarket, or at the laundromat waiting for their clothes to dry, or in the airport, wherever...they read everything in sight? Like the back of the cereal box during breakfast? Or, you can be waiting in the dentist's office for your scheduled treatment and you'll pick up a magazine entitled, Dentists Monthly and studiously peruse an article entitled 'Post-Operative Care of Crowns and Canals?' It's better than sitting there and doing nothing, don't you agree?"

Wormwood nodded.

"You can even be sitting on the can in the public restroom staring at all the graffiti etched on the door. Anything to read. Know what I'm saying?"

Wormwood almost nodded in agreement, but instead pursed his lips thoughtfully.

"That's the whole idea behind our new product," said Jimmy. "People read anything while they're waiting for something. It gives them a sense of accomplishment. And so we're considering introducing a line of toilet paper that has articles from the New York Times printed on it. How do you think that will go over?"

Wormwood coughed, then blew his nose. "Does it have to be the New York Times?"

"Of course not. But it's familiar to everybody. We think it's better than the Portland Oregonian or the Long Beach Press-Telegram. We're certainly open for suggestions, though, Mr. Wormwood. What are your thoughts?"

"What would you call the product?" Wormwood tried to look serious.

"That's the hard part. The Rap Wrap name for our school supply products has gone over so well, we've been trying to come up with a dynamite name that could equal it, if possible. In fact, we've come up with a couple. Those are what I would especially like to get your opinion about."

"Are the names available?"

"I can reveal them to you right now."

"Go ahead."

"I really appreciate your interest, Mr. Wormwood. Thank you. Even though we've come up with several dozen prospective names, we've reduced them down to two finalists. When I relate them to you, keep in mind the true function of toilet paper."

"Naturally."

"We've been torn between these two names. We can't decide whether to call the new product Ripe-Wipe...or Crap-Wrap."

Wormwood almost choked. Then he began to laugh. He laughed harder. He laughed so hard that tears began rolling down his cheeks. His whole boring career came down to this moment. The tedious, long days suffering through lengthy, pompous presentations from stuffed shirts all seemed less miserable now because of the exhilaration of this very moment, this letting loose...something he'd never done before.

"Wait right here, Jimmy," he finally exclaimed. "Don't move. I want the president of the company to hear this. I'll be right back."

* * *

Jimmy sold tons of product to that company for many years. Not toilet paper, of course, but school supplies. Jimmy sent Wormwood a customized sample, though, that Jimmy's artist produced. Jimmy learned that he kept it in his credenza and brought it out each time he repeated the story...hundreds of times.

Jimmy's presence lingered there for many years...after just one visit!

The Fifth W is not intangible, unreachable, mysterious, or illusive. It's the result of conscious effort, preplanning, and a striving to be different, outstanding, and memorable. Remember the garbage truck in the Rose Bowl parade, the poor cow at Doverland Milk, the Head of Lettuce, the banana hanging by a frayed string, the high school boy in Mr. Gray's mind, the red-headed job applicant, Mr. Principal's compulsion to break rules, and the final names for the toilet paper? Some are objects, some are ideas, some are thoughts or approaches; but all contain The Fifth W.

What are you thinking of?

* * *

Pop Quiz

1. Which of your neighbors would be asked to appear on the Tonight Show?
2. Recall an episode in your life that had people clamoring for more.
3. List the qualities that make your doctor or dentist so special.
4. What qualities did your favorite teacher possess?
5. What's your greatest idea? What caused others to like it?
6. What qualities does your favorite professional athlete possess?
7. What's your most outstanding event in the past two months?
8. List two goals that you're striving for.
9. Has the local newspaper ever done a story about you?

What will you do this week to develop Wow?

Chapter Two

Pulling the String

High Pressure

Think of the last thing you purchased or agreed to do. Did you do it because someone was stuffing it down your throat with high pressure tactics? Of course not. When people are pressured, they have a natural tendency to back away. Does that help them realize they want something? Of course not. It creates an awareness that one does not want it. Consequently, if high pressure causes people to back away, it's misguided to use it, because it only causes people to not want something.

High pressure, anyway, is a misnomer. When the seller cannot cause any consequences to occur other than the withdrawal of an item for sale if the prospect will not buy, then there can be no so-called high pressure.

Here's a list of possibilities where high pressure can exist:

1. The house you want to rent is the only one available in the entire area.
2. You must pay fifteen hundred dollars by 5 p.m. today. You're one thousand short.
3. You're buying a fire extinguisher while your house is on fire.
4. A stranger with a gun asks you for a donation.

At least one of three ingredients are each situation:

1. Immediate need
2. Limited supply
3. Force

Force is undesirable because it causes retreat. Some would say two other items should be added to the list...time and insistence. Time is subjective. It's almost always arbitrarily applied in a selling situation. When a furniture store ad claims, "Save 25%! Sale ends Monday!", who is under pressure? Where is the pressure? Are you all out of furniture? Are the furniture manufacturers going to stop production? Will no other store ever again have a sale? Is force involved? Advertisers recognize that time is a motivator, since it helps to urge prompt action. But it's not pressure in this context. Consumers keep falling for it, though. That's why it's such a common advertising tactic.

Insistence is something that individual salespeople use according to personality, but any resulting high pressure is self-imposed by the prospect who is unwilling or unassertive enough to retreat from the situation with a simple, "I'm not interested."

What causes a person to know that he wants something is for him to reach out for it. If he doesn't, he doesn't know he wants it. Persuasion or selling does not necessarily mean convincing someone to like something, but is instead putting the person in touch with his own desire for something.

Many salespeople play the aggressor...shoving facts and reasons to buy down the prospects' throats. As a result, prospects spend so much of their time defensively backing away from the onslaught that they never realize they actually do want what the salesperson is forcing on them. Nor do they learn about it.

The exact opposite of stuffing it down your throat is another high profile sales tactic...Pulling the String.

* * *

Ball of Yarn

Wiggle a Ball of Yarn with one end dangling in front of a kitten, and the kitten will have a natural, overwhelming desire to possess it. A little boy controlling the yarn will soon discover that the more the kitten cannot reach it, the more it will want it. When the little boy drops the yarn on the floor, though, the kitten will run to it, investigate briefly, and shortly thereafter ignore it.

Kittens do not have an exclusive on this natural behavior. Human beings are afflicted, too. If they weren't, salespeople would be order-takers, and persuasion would be unnecessary. When the kitten reaches out for the ball of yarn, it knows it wants it, or why would it be reaching out? His reaching out is what causes him to know he wants it, and the act of reaching out is caused by Pulling the String. Some people believe that it is what a salesperson says about a product or service that sells it. That's wrong. What causes a prospect to know that he wants something is his own action of reaching out for it.

If the little boy makes it too easy for the kitten to possess the ball of yarn, the kitten may never know how much it wants it. Desire is not caused by too much...but rather by not enough. The more available the product or service, the less desirable it becomes. If you are a male who has been stranded on a deserted island for two years, and suddenly a female appears, she'll probably seem very attractive, even if she's homely. But what happens if you're a nightclub owner who is surrounded every night by dozens of beautiful dancers, and that homely island girl appears?

* * *

Nylon Sale

In late 1945, a large, downtown department store advertised a sale on nylon stockings. During the war, nylon stockings were not available at any price because of material shortages. The night before the sale, women eagerly began queuing up in front of the store. By eight-thirty the following morning, hundreds were waiting for the store to open. Police were called to control the crowd. At nine o'clock, worried store officials unlocked the doors. Within minutes, the shoving, jostling, screaming, frantic horde of women had grabbed every available package of nylons from the store's shelves...and from each other. Whether they were the right size did not matter.

* * *

Love Story

Fred and Alice had been seeing each other steadily for two years...steadily for Alice, not necessarily for Fred. It wasn't a matter of

Fred stepping out on Alice or anything like that; it was just that Fred's bowling league, fishing trips, and poker parties took up a lot of his time…without Alice.

She was a sweet girl. And patient. Alice had marriage on her mind, and although they'd discussed it many times, Fred always found a way to put it off. Alice displayed a willingness to wait…and wait…and wait. Fred knew it. Whenever Fred called her, she was ready to drop everything to be with him. Fred knew that, too.

One day Fred tried unsuccessfully to phone Alice at her apartment. He tried constantly throughout the day and early evening. No answer. Fred got so worried that he hurried to her apartment. He saw a small envelope taped to the door with his name written on it. With shaking hands, he opened the envelope and read the note inside.

It read,

Dearest Fred,

I've always loved you. But I've waited too long. I am moving to another state. Do not try to find me. I have left no forwarding address. There is no way you can reach me. I love you.

Goodbye,
Alice

Fred stared at the note for several minutes, reading it over and over. Finally, he sat down on the porch outside the door, put his face in his hands and wept.

*　　　*　　　*

Buying a Dress

The dress was nice but Gloria Goodshape couldn't make up her mind. She'd tried it on, taken it off, tried it on again, taken it off, and she was now standing in front of the full-length mirror near the store entrance holding the dress in front of herself. A very gentle and patient saleswoman stood with her.

"I just don't know," Gloria said aloud. "I can't make up my mind."

Reflected in the mirror, Gloria spotted an attractive woman and a male companion watching her from across the shop. "Perhaps I'll look around some more and come back later."

Before the saleswoman could respond, the man walked over to Gloria and asked, "What size is that garment?"

"What?" replied Gloria.

"What size is that dress you're holding?"

The saleswoman interrupted, "It's a size seven."

"I was hoping it was. It's perfect. Please excuse me for interrupting." The man walked away toward the attractive woman, who was watching them.

Gloria turned to face the saleswoman. "How many of these dresses do you have?"

"That's the only one in any size."

"I see," said Gloria, turning back to the mirror to look once again. "It is quite becoming, don't you agree?"

"Very becoming, indeed."

"I believe I'll take it."

After Gloria departed with her new dress, the attractive woman and her male companion approached the saleswoman.

"I'm sorry, but the young lady purchased the dress I believe you were interested in," she said. "It was the only one we had."

"I know," said the man. "We watched her. We aren't interested in that dress."

"You aren't?"

"No. When the kitten reaches out for the yarn, she knows she wants it."

"Kitten?" asked the saleswoman.

"If she put that dress back on the rack, she knew it wouldn't be there when she returned. The fear of losing it to us caused her to know she wanted it. She reached out and possessed it."

The attractive woman laughed cheerfully and held her hand out to the saleswoman. "Jimmy does this all the time. Hello, I'm Susan Dover. Even though I'm not interested in that dress, there are a couple of outfits over here that I'd like to try on."

Everyone smiled. Help like that was hard to find.

* * *

In none of the three situations was high pressure used. There was either an immediate, compelling need or a short supply. The string was pulled, causing the object to be irresistible.

In Nylon Sale, the shortage of nylons was so widespread and acute that hundreds of women ached for some and acted like cattle to get them. The string had been pulled long before the sale. The string is defined as the availability of nylon stockings. There were none for several years. When the announcement was made by the department store that some were finally available, hundreds of women lunged at the string and grabbed whatever they could. Even nylons that were the wrong size were desirable to them.

Love Story is similar, but here the string is defined as the availability of Alice. When she was available, Fred didn't realize he loved her. When she was suddenly unavailable, Fred realized he did love her. His reaching out for the missing Alice was what caused that realization. Regardless of how the story evolves from that point, the effect is the same. If Fred manages to find Alice and asks her to marry and live happily ever after with him, his action will have been caused by Alice Pulling the String. Even if Fred does not manage to find Alice, he'll still realize he loves her.

In Buying a Dress, as soon as Gloria discovered that there was a short supply and that someone else also desired the dress, she knew she wanted it. Jimmy came over and tugged on the string. Gloria wouldn't let go. She gripped it tighter, and then bought it.

What if none of these people had reached for the string? What if no women had shown up for the Nylon Sale? It would simply mean that nobody wanted nylons, even if they were in short supply. What if Fred had not missed Alice when she left? Then it would seem that Alice was wise to leave anyway, because she was just wasting her time with Fred. And what if Gloria had put the dress back on the rack? Same thing. It would mean she didn't want the dress, because even the fear of losing it wouldn't cause her to buy it.

*　　　*　　　*

Did it take any courage for Alice to leave? She probably thought so at the time. Having the Guts to Fail is what helped get Alice's relationship with Fred out of neutral…an unsatisfactory status quo for them both. When one truly understands the dynamics of Guts to Fail, it no longer takes courage to Pull the String. What are you thinking of?

*　　　*　　　*

Guts to Fail

"This isn't a bad program, Jimmy," said Steve Stroker, the owner's son. "You've put in a lot of hard work on it. It's not bad."

The top of Steve's desk was crowded with materials for "The Straight Shooter" syndicated advertising campaign, which included cassette tapes, newspaper ad layouts, artwork, storyboards, radio copy, point-of-purchase signs, the works. For the past forty-five minutes, he'd listened to Jimmy Dover's presentation. It was 10:45 a.m., and Jimmy's next appointment was at 11:30. Jimmy knew it would take him twenty minutes to get there. Two other appointments were scheduled for that afternoon for the same campaign. Whoever said yes first got it. Jimmy didn't care who. Checks from any of them converted to legal tender at the bank.

"Thanks a lot," replied Jimmy. "I really appreciate your kind words, Steve. I take them as a personal compliment."

Whenever Jimmy went to a new city to sell his campaign, he always scheduled a minimum of ten appointments spread over three or four days. He knew for certain that he'd sell it if he made at least ten appointments. Often, he sold it to the first prospect, but in those cases he had the happy problem of phoning the remaining nine and informing them that the appointment needed to be canceled, which caused the prospect to be more desirous, not less, of seeing Jimmy, a common result of Pulling the String.

Jimmy had sold the campaign dozens of times throughout three countries. He observed one common trait in all his clients. If they weren't doing a tap dance on the desk within the first twenty minutes or so, they didn't like the campaign. And Steve was either a good actor or he didn't like it. People who like something don't talk condescendingly about it unless they're trying to hide their true feelings. Steve's comment, "This isn't a bad program. It's not bad," was the epitome of condescension. And when a person speaks like that, it's not the proper moment to ask for an order. Jimmy realized that for Steve to know he liked the campaign, he'd need to reach out for the string.

"You know, Steve," said Jimmy, "there are literally dozens of businesses like yours around the country that use this campaign. I've discovered one thing that's common to all of them, and I'm going to tell you what it is. When they saw this program the first time, they knew they liked it so much that they were tap dancing on the desk at this point of the presentation. It's what they'd been looking for for years. But you aren't doing that, Steve, so there's the distinct possibility that this campaign may not be for you."

Steve stared at Jimmy and said nothing.

Jimmy continued. "And that's really okay. After all, a person can't like everything! Besides, I have eight or nine other appointments in the next couple of days, and I always find a home for my program before I leave town."

As Jimmy spoke, he leaned forward and picked up his cassette player. The electric cord was plugged in beside the desk. Jimmy reached down and with some difficulty attempted to unplug it.

"Everyone has a different way of showing how he feels," said Steve as he watched Jimmy struggle to unplug the machine.

"Of course, of course. That's certainly true," replied Jimmy without looking at Steve. He was preoccupied with the plug on the cassette player. "I can't seem to get this out. I think it's stuck or something."

"Maybe I can get it," said Steve as he walked around the desk and stooped down next to Jimmy. He reached for the plug. "It is kind of tight, isn't it? There! I got it."

"Thanks a lot. Thanks a lot." Jimmy wrapped the cord around the cassette player and set it on the floor next to his chair. "Holy mackerel!"

Jimmy looked at his wristwatch. "I'm almost late for my next appointment!" He began picking up the ad layouts from Steve's desk and stacked them in a pile. "I hope I'm not forgetting anything. Got to have all my stuff, you know. Let's see. My ads. My book. Got my tape player. I sure am appreciative for all the time you've given me today, Steve. Thank you very much. Hope I don't get lost. I'm not real familiar with the city."

If Jimmy leaves now, Steve won't need to think about the campaign. There'll be nothing to think about. Jimmy will have sold it to someone else shortly. Naturally, if Steve does not like the campaign, it won't bother him for Jimmy to leave. But, Steve does like it. He's merely trying to act like he doesn't.

Steve appeared bewildered. He watched in seeming disbelief at Jimmy's preparation for retreat. He couldn't believe that someone would walk out on as much interest as he thought he was showing in the campaign. He realized that if he didn't stop Jimmy in the next ten seconds, he'd never have another opportunity before that particular campaign was purchased by someone else.

"Can I keep some of these layouts so that I can show them to my managers?" asked Steve.

"Oh gosh, if you do that, I'll be out of business for awhile. Those are the only ones I have, and I need them for my next appointments."

"I wouldn't need them for very long."

"That would make it difficult for me, Steve, it really would. But I'll tell you what. We are plotting and scheming new ideas for advertising campaigns and promotions all the time, and we are working on one right now that'll be dynamite! Listen. Next time I visit this city in six, eight, nine months from now, possibly a year, why don't I just plan to show you that one? It's going to be really really good."

Steve coughed. He wasn't interested in an invisible campaign that didn't exist. He liked the one he was looking at. Jimmy knew he liked it because Steve was reaching out for it. Jimmy kept pulling the string just beyond his grasp.

Jimmy opened his case and placed the artwork in it, then looked around the office to see what else was his. "Yes, that could very well be our best one ever."

Steve stood up abruptly. He looked disconcerted. He picked up the phone, listened, dialed two numbers, then put down the receiver impulsively. "Wait right here. Don't leave! I'll be right back!"

Jimmy said nothing. He sat quietly in the chair and watched Steve exit. Steve looked like he needed to collect his thoughts, as conducting business wasn't supposed to be like this. The seller was supposed to act like he wanted the buyer to buy (that's how one negotiates for a lower cost and added value).

Let's review this conversation and see what has occurred.

* * *

Steve:

"This isn't a bad program, Jimmy. You've put in a lot of hard work on it. It's not bad."

Steve is acting polite. Even though his tone of voice may not be condescending, his words indicate otherwise. A compliment containing a negative is often indicative of condescension. For example, "This isn't a bad house" could avoid condescension by simply substituting the negative with a positive, "This is a great house!" Instead of, "This isn't a bad program, Jimmy," Steve could have said, "This is a very fine program."

Some prospects disguise their true feelings by using the negative. Of course, some of them don't know how strongly they desire something until they reach out for it.

At this point, if Jimmy asked Steve to buy the program, he'd be asking him to buy something that was "not bad." Alternately, if Jimmy can get Steve to reach out for the program, he'll be asking him to buy something Steve knows he wants.

Jimmy:

"Thanks a lot. I really appreciate your kind words, Steve. I take them as a personal compliment. You know, Steve, there are literally hundreds of businesses like yours around the country that use this campaign. I've discovered one thing that's common to all of them, and I'm going to tell you what it is. When they see this program the first time, they know they like it so much that they're doing a tap dance on the desk at this point of the presentation. It's what they've been looking for for years. And you don't seem to be doing this, Steve, so there's the distinct possibility that this campaign may not be for you."

Jimmy is showing Steve that the ball of yarn is within his reach right now. But, if he won't reach out for it, Jimmy will pull it away. Steve must show interest now. If he doesn't, it means he's not afraid to lose the campaign.

Jimmy:

"And that's really okay. After all, a person can't like everything! Besides, I have eight or nine other appointments in the next couple of days, and I always find a home for my program before I leave town."

Jimmy is exhibiting the Guts to Fail. He's also indicating that there are many kittens who may be interested in his ball of yarn. When a prospect likes something, it's easy for him to believe that others will like it, too. Conversely, when a prospect dislikes something, he'll expect others to dislike it. Jimmy is giving Steve an opportunity to reach out for the campaign (the string), but if he doesn't, others will have that opportunity before Steve has a second chance. Jimmy physically pulls the string by removing the campaign from the desk and packing up.

Steve:

"Everyone has a different way of showing how he feels,"

Steve is getting in touch with his own desire for the campaign. His comment is a strong buying signal. He knows he must indicate some interest, but he wants to retain some bargaining position, so his initial show of interest appears weak. Jimmy requires a strong show of interest.

He ignores the weak showing. If the kitten feebly waves at the string, that's not nearly as persuasive as lunging at it.

Jimmy:

"Of course, of course. That's certainly true. I can't seem to get this out. I think it's stuck or something."

Jimmy continues to Pull the String. Steve must reach out for it if he's interested. Physically! It's now or never.

Steve:

"Maybe I can get it. It is kind of tight, isn't it? There! I got it."

He wants to touch something, to be involved. He must reach out to do that. But since touching is not the same as grabbing, Jimmy continues to pull the string.

Jimmy:

"Thanks a lot. Thanks a lot. Holy mackerel! I'm almost late for my next appointment! I hope I'm not forgetting anything. Got to have all my stuff, you know."

Steve wishes Jimmy would leave everything there. The vanishing campaign is becoming more and more irresistible. Jimmy risks nothing by pulling the string.

Jimmy:

"Let's see. My ads. My book. Got my tape player. I sure am appreciative for all the time you've given me today, Steve. Thank you very much. Hope I don't get lost. I'm not real familiar with the city."

Jimmy appears to be in full retreat. Steve will have to start chasing (lunging) to stop him. Steve is struggling to find a way to slow Jimmy down without having to grab him and nail him to the chair. The moment of truth has arrived. His own state of mind is what will cause Steve to know he loves the campaign and can't live without it. Nothing that Jimmy has said about the campaign has caused that to happen. Don't forget, Jimmy is retreating! Steve is the one reaching out.

Steve:

"Can I keep some of these layouts so that I can show them to my managers??"

Steve wants control. If he has the campaign in his possession to show the managers, then Jimmy won't have it to show to someone else.

Jimmy:

"Oh gosh, if you do that, I'll be out of business for awhile. Those are the only ones I have, and I need them for my other appointments."

Jimmy acknowledges he can't give up control. He continues to Pull the String.

Steve:

"I wouldn't need them for very long."

Steve implies that he'll make a fast decision if he can only get the campaign for a short while. He strives to sell Jimmy on how fast he can make a decision. Jimmy didn't ask him to make a fast decision…Steve simply volunteers. Why would Steve try to sell anything to Jimmy at this point if he didn't know he liked and wanted the campaign?

Let's not lose sight of another important point. Whose campaign is it? It's Jimmy's! Can Steve present the campaign better to the managers than Jimmy? Of course not! Yet, Steve asks if Jimmy will let him present the campaign to his managers. In its logical extreme, Steve is asking Jimmy if the least qualified presenter can show the campaign to the managers…almost preordained failure. Jimmy isn't crazy. No sane salesperson would allow that to happen. Also, no sane salesperson would allow control to get away from him in that way. One of Jimmy's options is to suggest that he'd be willing to present the campaign to the managers, but Jimmy has instead made the judgment that Steve has not lunged for the string yet, so he continues his present course.

Jimmy:

"That would make it difficult for me, Steve, it really would. But I'll tell you what. We are plotting and scheming new ideas for advertising campaigns and promotions all the time, and we are working on one right now that will be dynamite! Listen. Next time I come to this city in six, eight, nine months from now, possibly a year, why don't I just plan to show you that one? It's going to be really really good."

Offering a non-existent alternative is an excellent way to test a prospect's interest. At the same time, it allows Jimmy another opportunity to pull the string and act like he's ignoring Steve's booming interest while continuing his retreat.

Jimmy:

"Yes, that could very well be our best one ever."

Steve's brain turns to spaghetti. He can no longer pretend not to like the campaign by remaining passive. Lunging is required! He grabs the string with bewildering behavior.

Steve:

"Wait right here. Don't leave! I'll be right back!"

Who's in control now? Certainly not Steve. When the little boy dangles the string in front of the kitten, is the kitten in control of the situation, or the little boy? Pulling the String is such a potent high profile sales tactic that those readers who master it can have unimaginable magnetism. Be reminded, though, that this technique requires an unwavering adherence to the Guts to Fail tactic; and naturally, no technique can help if the person with whom you are dealing doesn't like what you're offering. Let's not leave Steve yet, though. There's more.

*　　　　*　　　　*

Three minutes went by. Steve returned, walked to his desk and faced Jimmy.

"Can you come back after six o'clock and meet with my managers?"

"Tonight?"

"Yes."

"After six?"

"Yes."

"How many would there be?"

"Four. My general manager, the sales manager, myself, and oh, my father said he'd like to be here, too."

"Your father?"

"Yes. I pretty much run the business, as I told you, but he comes in occasionally, and I don't believe he'd want to miss this."

Jimmy knew that whenever a prospect said anything positive, the salesperson must have the prospect repeat it by asking about it. Steve appeared to believe that he was doing something very nice by arranging the meeting...as though it were Steve's idea. Jimmy caused this plan to develop by Pulling the String. Jimmy continued to ask Steve to repeat the positive things.

"He wouldn't?"

"He happens to be in town this week."

Jimmy frowned. He reached into his jacket pocket and pulled out a piece of paper. He unfolded and looked at a list of his appointments.

"Six o'clock. Six o'clock. I don't know." Jimmy exhaled a huge sigh and scratched the top of his head. "I have another appointment at four o'clock. I think it's all the way across town."

"Forget your other appointment!" said Steve. After a beat he spoke more softly.

"I'm your best prospect right now. I like the campaign. I'll probably buy it. I just want to be certain my managers like it. Why don't you call and cancel your appointment, and I'll see that everyone is here at six o'clock?" Steve picked up the telephone and handed it to Jimmy. "I'll dial the number for you."

"You'll dial the number for me?"

"Of course."

"Right this second?"

"Why not?"

"Well, okay." Jimmy fumbled with his list and finally read the phone number aloud for his four o'clock appointment. Steve dialed.

Fait accompli! Who is selling whom? Steve is selling Jimmy on his extreme interest! The irony is that Steve believes that he's not acting interested. Harmless-looking Jimmy is getting Steve's interest forced down his throat. Steve even believes he is in control!

Within five minutes or so Steve has gone from condescension ("It's not bad") to actively changing Jimmy's appointment schedule. And during that time, Jimmy hasn't added one new piece of information about the campaign itself. Pulling the String caused the change in Steve's attitude? It certainly wasn't because Jimmy stuffed the campaign down Steve's throat or made it easy to get. Jimmy made it difficult to get, and Steve had to reach out for it. Steve sold himself on how much he wanted the campaign by his action of reaching out. If he didn't want the campaign, why would he do that?

Jimmy could have mishandled it by giving Steve the layouts and other materials so that he could show them to his managers. To do that, Jimmy would have had to cancel his other appointments, because he would have no campaign to show them. Each concession he made would have lowered the value of the program in Steve's eyes. If Jimmy had given Steve the program materials and canceled his other appointments, it's possible that Steve could have had the negative thought: "Jimmy doesn't think he can sell this to anybody else in this city. I wonder what's wrong with it?" But Jimmy held his ground, and every concession he did not make made the campaign more valuable to Steve.

The holder of the string has control. If he allows the prospect to grab the string too easily, it won't have much value. But, what about the other end of the string? What if you are the kitten and someone else is controlling the string? Suppose the kitten doesn't reach out for it? What would the little boy do if he was purposely trying to get the kitten to reach out for it? He might bring it closer to the kitten, thereby revealing his own desire for the kitten to have it. A reverse, isn't it? What if the kitten still doesn't reach out for it?

In the next story, Jimmy Dover finds himself at the other end of the string.

* * *

The Other End of the String

"Why don't you and Mrs. Dover go across the street and have a nice dinner and come back in an hour," said Barry Berry. "I'll phone and tell them you're coming. You're my guests."

Barry Berry stood up from his desk and moved toward his office door. Following his lead, Jimmy and Susan Dover stood up.

"That's very kind," said Jimmy.

"Will an hour give you enough time for dinner?" asked Barry. "Make it an hour and a half if you like."

"Is an hour suitable for you?" responded Jimmy.

"My partner, Perry is at our other office. I just want to chat with him for a few minutes about this. I'm sure he'll like the proposition. Take whatever time you need."

"We'll return here in an hour," said Jimmy.

"Ask the receptionist to ring me. "

Because Jimmy traveled so much, he made it a practice to take family members with him on sales trips, whenever possible. His wife, Susan, accompanied him frequently throughout the year. His children, one at a time, went during summer vacations. This practice provided a triple benefit: it gave him private, uninterrupted time with each child; it gave his kids new and unusual experiences; and it disarmed prospects when he showed up for an appointment with his wife or one of his kids.

Jimmy had invited Susan to go with him on this trip to Canada, and she'd looked forward to it for several weeks. It wasn't the shopping or hotels or lollygagging around the pool that attracted her interest so much as the opportunity to be with Jimmy and watch him work.

For the past two hours Jimmy had presented "That Magnificent Man & His Driving Machines" syndicated advertising campaign to Barry Berry, who appeared to like it. He said he wanted to get a go-ahead confirmed by his partner, Perry, who was involved in all money matters. It was six o'clock when he extended the dinner invitation.

During the meal, Susan remarked that it looked like a certainty that Barry would buy the program. In an hour they were back. Jimmy approached the receptionist's desk.

"Hello again. Will you let Mr. Berry know that we're back?"

"I'm sorry, Mr. Dover," said the receptionist, "but I believe Mr. Berry has left for the day."

She stared at Jimmy. Jimmy stared back. Susan stared at both of them.

"Would you care to leave a message for him?" asked the receptionist.

Jimmy coughed. "We'd arranged to meet with him here at seven o'clock. Will you ring his office or page him to be certain he has left?"

She dialed and listened. "Oh! Mr. Berry! You're still here! I'm sorry, sir, I thought you'd left. Mr. and Mrs. Dover are here. What? Oh. Yes. I'll tell them." She put down the phone and looked up at Jimmy. "He said if you'd care to wait, he'll be with you in a few minutes. You may sit right over there if you like."

Jimmy and Susan sat down and waited.

The other end of the string is the one the kitten reaches for. The roles were switched. Barry Berry had the string firmly in his grasp, and Jimmy found himself reaching out for it.

As he waited with Susan, Jimmy had no particular thought other than if Barry chose not to like the program, he wouldn't buy it. If he did like it, but pretended not to, Jimmy would need to utilize the Guts to Fail, take possession of the string and pull it away, so that Barry would need to reach out for it. The Dovers waited for nearly fifteen minutes. Finally, Barry emerged from his inner sanctum and approached them.

"How was dinner?" he asked.

Jimmy stood up. "That alone was worth the trip."

"Glad you enjoyed it." Barry peered at his watch. "Well, you might as well come into my office for a minute."

They followed him into his office. Susan looked like her optimism had vanished. Barry stood behind his desk and hesitated, then motioned for them to sit down.

"Be seated and I'll tell you what happened," he said as he sat down, too. Obviously, bad news was imminent. Jimmy began thinking about his appointment schedule for the following day.

"I got Perry on the phone," said Barry. "I outlined the campaign and your proposition, and he sort of liked it."

Jimmy smiled faintly.

"Of course," continued Barry, " he couldn't see all the print ad layouts, but he depends on my judgment for that." He paused and looked down at his hands, which were clasped together on top of his desk. He stared at Jimmy, frowned, and looked down at his hands again. Susan sat motionless.

As Jimmy eyed him, he recalled a movie scene in which the doctor was getting ready to tell the patient he had terminal cancer and would be dead in less than a week.

Barry continued. "The biggest concern that Perry had about your proposal, Jimmy, is the fact that after we've used the program for one year, your licensing agreement requires us to pay a renewal fee if we choose to continue its use for a second year."

"Your explanation sounds right," replied Jimmy.

Barry stared at Jimmy for several seconds if though waiting for him to say more. Jimmy added nothing. Susan stared at the desk paraphernalia. Barry leaned back in his chair.

"Is there some way you can alter that requirement?" asked Barry. "That's the bugaboo that bothers Perry about your proposal."

Barry was dangling the string in front of Jimmy. He obviously wanted Jimmy to eliminate the one year term and make it longer...or cancel the renewal fee. He implied that he'd buy the campaign, with Perry's blessing, if Jimmy would cede that condition. But Jimmy wanted the term to stick, and he knew he needed to convince Barry that he felt the one year requirement was more important than whether or not Barry bought the campaign.

Jimmy leaned forward in his chair, picked up his briefcase, and set it on his lap. "I wish I could say yes to that, but I can't. As soon as I begin manipulating the terms of my own program, for any reason at all, it will be all over for me. I'll be out of business. If you chose to continue my program in the second year, that would mean it had value to you, it was doing its job, and it was worth the renewal amount. I'm sorry. I can't alter that requirement."

Barry sighed and leaned forward. He stared at Jimmy plaintively. Jimmy stared back. Susan remained still. Barry rose from his seat. Jimmy started to stand, too, acting as though Barry was indicating that they leave.

"No, don't get up yet," said Barry. "Just a minute."

Jimmy sat down. Barry walked to the window and looked out at the darkness. He returned to his chair, sat down, swiveled around toward the wall and opened the drawer in his credenza. He pulled out a file, looked at it vacantly, returned it to the drawer, closed it, swiveled his chair around to face the Dovers, leaned forward on his desk, then clasped his hands together thoughtfully.

"Are you absolutely certain of that, Jimmy?" he asked.

"Yes. I'm sorry to say."

Without further hesitation, Barry replied. "I figured as much, Jimmy, and that's what I told Perry. We've decided to go ahead with your program. We both like it very much."

The reverse is complete. Barry, who started out holding the string, ended up reaching out for it. Jimmy had successfully regained control of it.

Let's see what occurred.

* * *

Barry:

"Why don't you and Mrs. Dover go across the street and have a nice dinner and come back in an hour. I'll phone and tell them you're coming. You're my guests."

Jimmy:

"That's very kind."

Barry likes the program very much, and he's offering an effective distraction to keep Jimmy from showing the program to a competitor while he consults with his business partner. A minor point is that sometimes a gift takes the edge off the seller's seeking the highest possible price. In effect, the prospect offers a hundred dollar dinner for a thousand dollar or more discount.

Barry:

"Will an hour give you enough time for dinner? Make it an hour and a half if you like."

Jimmy:

"Is an hour suitable for you?"

Barry wouldn't mind if Jimmy took four or five hours. Or even if he came back tomorrow. Barry doesn't realize he's reaching for the string. Jimmy does. Recognizing that the dinner offer connotes much interest by Barry, Jimmy opts for the shorter time choice, placing the burden on Barry to act faster.

Barry:

"My partner, Perry, is at our other office. I just want to chat with him for a few minutes about this. I'm sure he'll like the proposition. Take whatever time you need."

Barry is now selling Jimmy about how interested he is in the program, and how easy it will be to get his partner's blessing. In the same statement, Barry is begging Jimmy for more time.

Jimmy:

"We'll return here in an hour."

Jimmy declines the offer for more and keeps the pressure on Barry to act fast. Barry knows he wants the program, because he has bribed Jimmy to give him extra time, but he's shrewd enough to realize he must maintain his bargaining position. Even though Barry may not know the principle of Pulling the String, his next actions will, in effect, take possession of the string, putting Jimmy at the other end and causing Jimmy to do the reaching out.

Barry:

"Ask the receptionist to ring me."

(After returning from dinner)

Jimmy: (to receptionist)

"Hello again. Will you let Mr. Berry know that we're back?"

Receptionist:

"I'm sorry, Mr. Dover, but I believe Mr. Berry has left for the day. Would you care to leave a message for him?"

This is a shock disclosure to Jimmy and Susan. Whether Barry planned it or not, the effect is the same. Barry could have arranged for the receptionist to say he'd left, he could have gone through the act of leaving and sneaked back into his office through a side door; or the receptionist's belief that he'd left could be due to the late hour and a reasonable expectation on her part. Whatever caused it, the disclosure creates sharp disappointment and dismay for Jimmy, and he realizes then how much he wanted Barry to buy the program. So does Susan.

Barry now has the string in his possession. Jimmy must reach out for it. Jimmy suddenly finds himself on the other end of the string. If Barry arranged the situation, the reader may wonder whether he was taking a risk that Jimmy would depart and sell his program to a competitor before he could return the following day. The answer is no. Barry would have sized Jimmy up for what he was...a very bright and aggressive salesperson, one who would ask the receptionist to confirm that Barry had really left (which is just what he did). If that did not occur, then Barry would be smart enough to arrange to accidentally see Jimmy in the parking lot and walk back into the office with him.

Jimmy:

"We'd arranged to meet with him here at seven o'clock. Will you ring his office or page him to be certain he has left?"

Receptionist:

"Oh! Mr. Berry! You're still here! Mr. and Mrs. Dover are here to see you. What? Oh. Okay. Fine. Yes. I'll tell them." She put down the phone and looked up at Jimmy. "He said if you'd care to wait, he'll be with you in a few minutes. You may sit right over there if you like."

Waiting is not fun or productive for the waiter. As a purposeful ploy, it is not recommended. The writer considers it deceitful. Responsible persuasion must not include lack of courtesy. The following could have occurred with or without the wait.

Barry:

"How was dinner?

Jimmy:

"That alone was worth the trip."

Barry:

"Glad you enjoyed it."

Polite conversation. Cheerful greeting. The extreme contrast causes Jimmy to believe he may have been concerned over nothing. Perhaps Barry is interested after all. As elevators go up and down, so can interest...and people's emotions. This is called the Yo-yo Effect. First, Barry buys their dinner (much show of interest), then the receptionist announces he's gone (shattering disappointment), then Barry greets them as though everything's on track (interest again). The Yo-yo Effect can be very effective. Whip up the eggs and they become scrambled.

Barry:

"Well, you might as well come into my office for a minute."

The yo-yo is down again. Barry's statement sounds foreboding. The only redeeming feature implied is that Barry is enough of a gentleman to explain his turndown in the privacy of his office.

Barry:

"Be seated and I'll tell you what happened. I got Perry on the phone. I conveyed your proposition, and he sort of liked it. I played him the jingles. Of course, he couldn't see all the print ad layouts, but he depends on my judgment for that."

This is the moment of transition. It had appeared that Barry was no longer interested in the program, but now the opposite appears. The yo-yo is back up. Jimmy will control the string with the accompanying Guts to Fail.

Barry:

"The biggest thing that troubled Perry about your proposal, Jimmy, is the fact that after we've used the program for one year, your licensing agreement requires us to pay an annual renewal if we choose to continue using it."

Now the string is the program. When Jimmy returned from dinner, the string was Barry's interest. Barry had seemingly pulled it away, hoping to maintain some bargaining leverage. Barry wanted to eliminate the renewal provision. Jimmy controls the string now. If he pulls it away, the renewal provision will be attached. The Guts to Fail in this case is Jimmy not ceding that point to save the transaction. The author maintains that if Jimmy does cede, then Barry will find another objection, and another, and so on, until Jimmy gives away everything, and ultimately renders his program worthless.

Jimmy:

"You explained it to him correctly."

In poker, a player bets his hand, and takes no cards. His opponent can believe he has a pat hand or is bluffing. It's showdown time...Guts to Fail at work. Either player can back down. Barry blinks.

Barry:

"Is there some way you can alter that requirement? That's the bugaboo that bothers Perry about your proposal."

Barry lunges at the string by making a qualified offer to buy. Jimmy opts to add value rather than cede. When he pulls the string away, Barry's reaching out for it will cause Barry to know from his own action that the advertising campaign has much appeal and value to him.

Jimmy:

"I wish I could say yes to that, but I can't. As soon as I begin altering the terms of my own program for any reason at all, it will be all over for me. I'll be out of business. If you chose to continue my program after the first year, that would mean it had great value to you, it was doing its job, and it was worth the renewal cost. I'm sorry. I can't alter that requirement."

Jimmy must be convincing with his Guts to Fail response in the same way a good poker player must play his hand, even when he has poor cards. Any sign of weakness will bring poor results. The Guts to Fail means just that...guts! Barry still has an option to hold out for eliminating the renewal provision, but he elects not to.

Barry:

"Are you absolutely certain of that, Jimmy?"

Jimmy:

"Yes. I'm sorry to say. I really am."

Barry:

"I figured as much, Jimmy, and that's what I told Perry. We've decided to go ahead with your program. We both like it very much."

Victory! For whom? Everybody! Jimmy finds a home for his campaign without altering the terms, and Barry gets one that he loves and needs and is willing to pay for. Was there any high pressure? None that was obvious. It's a person's reaching out for something that creates the awareness that he wants it, causing the object of his reach to be irresistible. As demonstrated by Jimmy, the game can be played from the other end of the string, too. To master Pulling the String, one must be able to identify the string itself as well as his position as "puller" or "kitten." Then strive to obtain and maintain the control position.

Conversation, persuasion, selling form a mosaic...a tapestry of emotion, information, aggression, retreat, humility, silence, tact, technique, point, counterpoint, strength, and bluff. It's a verbal chess game. Pulling the String, Guts to Fail, and Yo-yo Effect are all high profile sales tactics in your repertoire.

Here's another.

* * *

Asking For a Turndown

It was 8 a.m., and the sales meeting was scheduled to begin. KPUK-AM/FM Radio had a sales staff of twelve representatives plus the sales manager, Doyle Peterson, who'd appeared thirty seconds earlier, accompanied by Jimmy Dover. Doyle Peterson was never late.

Nothing appeared to be different about this particular meeting...except that Jimmy was the station's guest this week to call on tough accounts.

"You all know Jimmy Dover from his last visit four months ago," said Doyle. "I just love the topic he's chosen to speak about today."

All stared at Jimmy. At least half of them had worked with him the last time he was in town making calls on clients. Art Goodsell recalled the meeting between Jimmy and the vice-president of advertising for the local bank. Art had been there. He'd been certain at the time that all were doomed, that the banker was not going to make a decision, that they were going to leave without an order; when suddenly the banker jumped up from his desk and demanded to buy the program on the spot.

That same evening, Art had attempted to explain to his wife what occurred, but he couldn't...he didn't know. What was most inexplicable to Art was that on previous occasions, the same banker had always claimed that he had to get approval from the bank's executive committee on any particular proposal, but this time the subject didn't come up.

"First," continued Doyle, "I want to go around the room quickly and find out what happened through last Friday. And to make this as fast as possible so that we can give most of the time to Jimmy, I will ask each of you for just a one word response. I'll start with you, Jason, and then go around the table clockwise."

In an instant, all twelve salespeople opened their briefcases and folders expecting to relate sales activity from last week.

"Last week, Jason," asked Doyle, "how many turndowns did you get?"

Jason stared at Doyle with a blank look. He looked down at his notes, then back at Doyle. A murmur went around the table as all looked at each other in wonder.

"How many turndowns?" asked Jason.

"Listening is not a lost art. Congratulations."

After a long pause, Jason stammered, "Well, uh…let me see, Monday I saw, uh…"

He looked up at the ceiling as though in deep concentration. "Then…well, I mean, on Tuesday, the, uh, shopping…well, they'll present at the promotion committee next…let's see, uh…"

"Come on, Jason," urged Doyle. "One word should describe how many turndowns you got last week."

"Well, Doyle," said Jason, "I can honestly say I didn't get any. You know, the bank deal was put off until Hammerstein returns from Tahiti…and the hardware store group will let me know a week from Thursday…then, of course, Charles Smith Realty is considering the weekend sports package, and their agency is probably going to give it the green light."

"Jason? If you didn't get any turndowns last week, just say zero. Okay?"

"Okay, Doyle. Zero." Jason emitted a long frustrated sigh.

"What about you, Cookie?"

"Actually, Doyle, I had a pretty good week. Lots of things cooking between now and the end of the month."

Doyle wagged his finger at her. "Are you searching for that word, too? Like Jason? Z-E-R-O?"

"Yes, Doyle. Zero. Zilch."

"What about you, Art?"

He was still thinking about the aberrant behavior of the banker, who'd indicated that he kind of liked the program, and that he'd take it up with the Executive Committee a week from Tuesday. He remembered that Jimmy stood up, moved to the door, and informed the banker that they needed to phone the station, in any event, to see if the program was still available; that only one bank could participate; and that they were already late for their next appointment.

Art recalled that Jimmy had said, "Rats. A week from next Tuesday will be too late. I'd like to suggest that you simply pass on this program, and just know that within the next two or three months the station will have another just as exciting. Hopefully, we'll have more warning than we had on this one. Finding out ourselves just two hours ago and then rushing over here hoping you'd snap it up really doesn't give you a chance…the way your approval system is set up. Please know, though, we brought it to you first. Art, we'd better be getting along now. Don't forget to phone Doyle Peterson and let him know the program is still available."

*   *   *

Asking for a Turndown is similar to Pulling the String. There was no guarantee that the banker would reach out…he certainly wouldn't if he didn't like it. Asking for a Turndown caused the banker to know he did like this program, which would not be available if he waited for his Executive Committee decision.

"Art!" yelled Doyle. "How many turndowns?

Art jerked out of his reverie and stared at Doyle…then at Jimmy.

"I get it. I get it," he exclaimed.

"That's three words," replied Doyle.

"I got a flat turndown from City Ford. People's Lumber turned down the Late Show package. And New Securities that just opened a branch in North County told me they're going to be all print for the foreseeable future."

"Okay," replied Doyle. "Three turndowns. Any others?

"That's it," said Art.

"Becky, what about you?

During the next three minutes Doyle asked each the same question. Nobody had any turndowns the previous week except Art. An incredible-sounding achievement. Assuming that each salesperson made an average of eight calls per day, then eights times five days times twelve salespeople equals four hundred eighty sales calls with only three turndowns! Astonishing! How could that be correct?

* * *

The concept that Jimmy intended to introduce to the sales staff was that if they could accept the premise that a turndown is a commitment, they would not be so hesitant to ask for one. That's right. A turndown is a commitment...a commitment not to do something. Prospects have a natural initial reluctance to make commitments; often they're just not mentally prepared. Asking for a Turndown exploits this reluctance.

Think about yourself, dear reader. Are you always mentally prepared to commit yourself when someone asks? Asking for a Turndown helps you recognize that you may desire the alternative because of your reluctance to say no. When someone asks you, "If you won't say yes, why don't you turn it down then?" your response could be, "I'm not ready to make a commitment." You might say to yourself, "I'm not ready to say yes or no." Turning something down does constitute a commitment. By refusing to say no, you're implying that you may want to say yes. That's how Asking for a Turndown works. As a prospect puts off a "no," he's acknowledging the possibility of a "yes." Conversely, if he's asked only for a "yes," his reluctance to make a commitment allows him only one answer..."no."

Let's return to the meeting.

* * *

"I'm turning the meeting over to Jimmy now," said Doyle. "Don't forget, he'll be here through Friday to make sales calls with us. Problem accounts only. You're up, Jimmy."

Was it Dr. Jekyll's turn? Or Mr. Hyde's? When Jimmy stood up, his chair teetered backward and fell with a thud on his opened briefcase.

Cassette tapes clattered onto the floor along with some loose papers and folders. Instantly, Jimmy was on his knees underneath the conference table, apologizing for the interruption and gathering his belongs with even more noise.

Art remembered that Jimmy had started the meeting at the bank the same way, with everything falling all over the floor. Everyone was stooped under the table to help him. They were witnessing another high profile sales tactic, Turn Into Columbo.

When someone comes across as being infallible, others have a tendency to look for flaws. Conversely, when things begin with evidence of human frailty, others are inclined to empathize and look for the good.

Watch a stereo buff buy new equipment? Criticism permeates his facial expressions as he asks negative questions and expects negative answers. He twists knobs, fiddles with switches, listens intently for pops, crackles, fade-outs. He's not looking for what's good about the equipment, but instead what isn't. How can these negative expectations be turned around? Isn't it better for someone to look for what they like instead of the opposite?

* * *

Homemade Family Room

Bill had spent two months working evenings and weekends remodeling his family room. He'd built bookshelves, hung the doors, installed new windows, and was proud of the results. So was his wife, Harriet. When Bill's older brother, Uncle George, stopped by for a visit, Harriet was eager to show him the new family room.

"Bill didn't know he had it in him," exclaimed Harriet. "But you know how your brother is. The challenge was there. He made the design, ordered the materials, and did all the work by himself. It's perfect. I'm dying for you to see it."

"Show me," replied Uncle George.

They walked down the basement stairs. Harriet turned on the light. George looked in, smiled and began to examine closely the molding around the door. He noticed a hairline crack between two pieces of mahogany and a shiny nail head that hadn't been set below the surface. He proceeded across the room to the bookshelves.

"This is Bill's work?" he asked.

"He's so proud of them."

"Mmm." George rubbed his fingertips across a shelf to see if it had been smoothly sanded. It felt rough to him. He stooped down and noticed that the bottom shelf didn't fit snugly against the back wall.

George wasn't interested in seeing how good Bill's was. He was more interested in finding imperfections.

Let's start this story over and see how Harriet could have created in George the need to seek the positive instead of the negative.

* * *

" Bill didn't know he had it in him," exclaimed Harriet. "But you know how your brother is. The challenge was there. He made the design, ordered the materials, and did all the work by himself. And now he doesn't want anyone to see it."

"Why not?" asked George.

"You know how Bill is. He's such a perfectionist. If it's not exactly right, it doesn't look good to him. He doesn't want anyone to see it until he thinks it's perfect. That could be months from now."

"I want to see it."

"We'll sneak a peek."

They walked down the basement stairs. Harriet turned on the light. George looked in, smiled, and turned to Harriet.

"This is fabulous. Do you think I could talk him into redoing my den?"

* * *

In the next situation, Jimmy Dover's advertising agency is soliciting a new account, a regional restaurant chain. Jimmy's agency is one of several that are making proposals to the assembled executives, over a two day period. Jimmy recognizes that his audience will be looking for imperfections because his agency is the smallest one making a pitch. Coming across as perfect, he believes, is ill-advised. It's time to Turn Into Columbo.

* * *

Imperfect Pitch

"Good morning," said Jimmy. "I had a problem getting here today. Driving to the airport with my wife and son, Josh, we had to stop at a pet shop to pick up a goldfish. They were all out of those plastic bags that close at the top, so they gave us the goldfish in a small bowl. Josh sat in the back seat holding onto it. And wouldn't you know it, as I was driving onto the expressway, I had to stop short, and the water sloshed all over the case I use to carry my cassette player and tapes. More than anything, everyone was more worried about the goldfish. It survived. I'm not so sure about my tape player, though. It may sound a little gurgly. It's the only one I've got. If you listen real carefully, I'm sure you'll get the idea. The first spot establishes the theme for the entire campaign."

Jimmy turned to the restaurant chain president, who sat beside him at the conference table. "By the way, you don't happen to have a cassette player, do you, just in case?"

"We're prepared," said the president.

"Well, don't get it yet. I think mine will work."

Jimmy lifted his cassette player out of the case, and as everybody stared at him, he set it atop the table.

"Let me move your water glass," said the president. He smiled.

"Thank you. I'll just make sure I've got the right tape. Just a second." He peered into his briefcase. "Yep...nope. It's this other one. I believe it's okay. Looks like the goldfish bowl missed it. Thank goodness.

Jimmy didn't appear to be talking to anyone in particular. He was preoccupied with the tape and cassette player. "I'll just put it in and turn it on."

He flipped a switch. It sounded like Donald Duck talking backwards.

"Oops. Hit the reverse. Sorry, that's not what it sounds like." Jimmy turned it off. "I do see a problem, though. The needle is indicating there's not much battery left. It'll probably be okay. We'll just find out, I guess. Here goes. By the way, this first spot requires no introduction. But the volume on my player doesn't go up very high, so we'll have to be real quiet while we listen. Ready?"

"When you are, Jimmy," answered the president. He smiled broadly.

The room was still. Each person leaned forward in eager anticipation. They sensed an urgency, a desire to hear the tape, to want to like what they heard. In less than three minutes, everybody had been converted from a bias against to a bias for. They were like a litter of kittens reaching out for a piece of yarn.

Jimmy was right. It was a good spot. Everyone liked it. In fact, they loved the whole campaign. Jimmy was right about something else, too. He couldn't start his presentation until they were ready to look for the good in it. When they were only seeking flaws, his presentation, no matter how good, would have failed.

When Jimmy finished, the president stood up. "Thank you, Jimmy," he said, "for your presentation. I want you to know I consider it to be very, very good. We've already heard from three other agencies. I learned a long time ago that it's easier to tone down too much creativity than it is to boost up mediocrity. I'm excited. I think we all are."

"Thank you," replied Jimmy.

"Gentlemen," said the president, "let's adjourn for thirty minutes and think about what we've seen and heard. We'll reconvene and make our choice. Jimmy, please stay behind for a few minutes. I want to chat with you about something. Let's give Jimmy a hand for his fine presentation."

"Good job," cried a voice from the end of the table as everyone clapped and exited. "Right!" responded another. The president closed the door and returned to Jimmy.

"There's something I've got to ask you, Jimmy, and well…I'd appreciate it very much if you'd give me a simple straightforward answer."

Jimmy shifted in his chair. "Naturally. What is it?"

"Remember now, just a short, simple answer."

"Of course."

"When you were fooling around with your own tape recorder, were you just pretending to be flustered, or did you really have trouble remembering how it worked?"

What a question! If Jimmy answers yes, he'll admit his Columbo "cover." If he answers no, he'll admit that he doesn't know how to operate his own equipment, which means he's really dumb.

"Well, sir," replied Jimmy, "when I first got…"

"Remember, Jimmy, a simple answer."

"I remember. And I will. But it took you almost half a minute to ask me. I know it'll take me at least half that time to answer."

"Okay."

"Let me answer this way. When I first got into this business not that long ago, I found myself working with equipment that I was unfamiliar with and discovered early on that some people found it entertaining to see me fumble around with everything. Yet they were still attentive and helpful. So, I made it a point to never get too familiar with my own equipment…or anyone else's."

The president's grin widened. "Just what I thought. That's beautiful!" He patted Jimmy's shoulder. "If your campaign can get our customers to reach out for our restaurants and products the way you got us to reach out for your presentation, we're going to have a winner."

*　　*　　*

Pop Quiz

1. List the three things that cause high pressure.
2. What causes a person to know that he wants something?
3. Define the string in:
a. Nylon Sale
b. Love Story
c. Buying a Dress
4. What caused Fred to weep in Love Story?
5. What caused Gloria Goodshape to buy the dress?
6. When did Barry Berry decide to buy Jimmy's campaign...before or after Jimmy went to dinner?
7. Why did Steve Stroker set up the six o'clock meeting?
8. Define the other end of the string.
9. Does Asking for a Turndown have anything to do with Pulling the String?
10. Think about the your most recent purchase costing more than $300. Did the salesperson believe you liked it a lot before you said you'd buy it? Did you act like you were not interested while you looked at it? Did you get a special deal? Why or why not?
11. If you're married, recall the reason the marriage proposal was made when it was. Why not the week before? A month later?
12. List five things that are desirable to you. Do you now possess them?

Chapter Three

Lofty Platitudes

We're bombarded with lofty platitudes. Communications are permeated with them. Amazingly, they almost always create a negative response.

A lofty platitude is a declarative sentence that contains a superlative or a grandiose description of the subject. Here are some examples:

1. Spokane, Washington is the greatest city in the United States.
2. Tennessee residents are smarter than other people.
3. Ajax Life Insurance Company has the best policy.
4. Chevrolet makes the most dependable vehicles and gives the most value.
5. My high school has the coolest kids.
6. It's our biggest sales event ever.
7. Save like never before.

Each example contains a categorical declaration that the subject is best. Reread the first one.

1. Spokane, Washington is the greatest city in the United States.

Suppose the reader lives and works in Des Moines and loves it there? Or Fort Lauderdale? Or Devils Lake? Or Anaheim? If so, won't the first example cause the reader to have a negative response? The thought may occur that Spokane isn't the greatest city...Anaheim is...or wherever the reader resides.

*　　　　*　　　　*

Fill in the Blanks

____________________is the greatest city in the United States.

When you say aloud the name you've indicated to someone living elsewhere, will the statement cause him to respond negatively?

Consider statement number two.

2. Tennessee residents are smarter than other people.

It may be well-received at a Chamber of Commerce meeting in Nashville, Lebanon, or Memphis; but what if someone declares it in a classroom in New Jersey or at a city council meeting in Florida?

____________________are smarter than other people.

Fill in the blank with the state or province you prefer. Say it aloud to someone who isn't from that state. Then find someone who is from that state, and say it aloud to him. Any difference?

This exercise may be repeated for all six statements. The results will be the same. Lofty platitudes cause negative responses...unless the receiver of the information is pre-sold on the subject. Since most people are not pre-sold about a subject they're not already familiar with, they'll give a negative response...or think one.

If one thousand people were selected at random, how many would be from Spokane, Washington (unless the selection was conducted in Spokane)? One? Two? Even if two, then nine hundred ninety eight out of one thousand will give a negative response to statement number one. Yet lofty platitudes permeate consumer advertising. Some very bright and creative people are highly-paid practitioners of the advertising business who constantly advocate and create lofty platitudes. Here are some. "America's favorite batter." "New and Improved...Our Best Cake Mix." "No Unhappy Owners." "Maintenance-free Dishwashers." "We won't be undersold." "We take better care of your car." Thousands of huge corporations and small companies spend billions of dollars advertising lofty platitudes that cause millions of consumers to have negative responses to their products and services. Here's another. "The On-Time Airline." If ever there was an advertising slogan guaranteed to create negative responses, this is it. How could it possibly succeed? An airline that is late even one percent of the time is risking many unhappy passengers when it advertises that it's never late!

Jimmy Dover knows all about lofty platitudes and recognizes them quickly in consumer advertising. Occasionally he has a little fun with them in an engaging sort of way.

*   *   *

We're Never Late...Sometimes

The airline ticket agent answered the phone and cheerfully announced, "Good morning, Mt. Airy Airlines, the On-Time Airline."

The caller was Jimmy Dover. "Is Flight 741 to Cleveland going to be on time?"

"No."

Imagine the frustration the airline employee feels every time he must disavow his own company's advertising slogan. An airline employee with an appealing personality may overcome the negative aspects of this impossible advertising promise. A call from Jimmy Dover can help, too. The conversation can be more interesting if the airline employee realizes the futility of his company's slogan, and a friendly dialogue commences. Let's start over.

The airline ticket agent answered the phone and cheerfully announced, "Good morning, Mt. Airy Airlines, the On-Time Airline."

"Is Flight 741 to Cleveland going to be on time?"

"No."

"I'll bet you'd like to say yes every time you're asked, in view of your company's advertising slogan, wouldn't you?"

"Yes, I really would. We're trying. We really are."

"Well, let me give you an opportunity to do that then."

"I'm all ears."

"Is Flight 741 going to be late?"

"Yes!...uh...that's not exactly the kind of yes I had in mind."

"I may have a remedy. What flight coming in sometime this morning do you already know will be on time?"

"Let me check. It looks like Flight 397 from Oklahoma City."

"When will you know for certain?"

"It's on final approach now."

"Then you're ready for the question?"

"Yes."

"Is Flight 397 from Oklahoma City going to be on time?"

"Yes."

"Feel better?"

"Yes."

Four yeses in a row are the most the ticket agent has given since the advertising slogan began. To repeat: billions of dollars are spent advertising lofty platitudes which cause millions of consumers to have negative responses to advertisers' products and services. The public has become jaded. Including children.

True, if a reader of a particular ad already buys that particular product or service, and he already loves it, then a lofty platitude will be acceptable. (Like telling a happy resident of Ft. Myers, Florida that Ft. Myers is the greatest; or informing a Dodgers fan that the Dodgers will win the pennant this year).

There is a psychological term for this behavior called Selective Perception. But since the expressed purpose of most advertising is to attract new customers, then the use of lofty platitudes in advertising is a huge waste of money. When the reader discovers himself using one orally, he should immediately prick it with a pin. For example, "This is the greatest new food discovery since sliced bread...but, oh well, in one hundred years from now, what difference will it make? Two hundred years anyway."

How often have you heard an acquaintance describe his doctor as "the best heart surgeon in the country?" (Or whatever his specialty happens to be). Keep in mind, there can only be one. During Monday Night Football, the announcers describe a player after each good play as the best one in the league at that position, followed by, "He should be going to the Pro Bowl this year." Are they all going? Keep in mind, this exaggeration continues several times per game...every week of the season. How many wide receivers can be "the best"? (Or whatever their positions may be). Logic mandates just one. Credibility plummets. Hyperbole reigns. When the reader begins a sentence with a lofty platitude, he must stop...and start over. Of course, he must be able to recognize lofty platitudes. In the following situation, Jimmy Dover demonstrates the use of one with a prospect who is in a big hurry.

*   *   *

The Greatest Shortest Story

Mr. Rush, the canned goods buyer, was in 'hurry up' mode. Jimmy was on time for his scheduled fifteen minute appointment with him at the grocery wholesaler.

"I'm sorry to rush you," said Mr. Rush, "but if you can take less than the allotted time, I will appreciate it. I have to drive across town later this afternoon. So, what is it?"

"I appreciate that, Mr. Rush, I really do," replied Jimmy. "I can do this in a flash." He set his sample case down in front of Mr. Rush's desk, and remained standing. "I want to tell you something right now that is really great...so great, in fact, that I can hardly believe it myself! The problem is that I have to use some lofty platitudes to explain it to you...because it really is great...and lofty platitudes usually create negative responses. I don't want to go to all the trouble to tell you about my wonderful idea if you're going to have a negative response."

"What is it?"

"It's here in my briefcase."

"Show me."

"Do you mind if set my case on your desk?"

"Let me move these papers."

Although Jimmy used a lofty platitude, he pricked it with a pin and warned Mr. Rush that he might have a negative response. That encouraged Mr. Rush to give Jimmy time to present his idea properly. Even if Mr. Rush doesn't like Jimmy's idea, it becomes more difficult for him to express a negative response after Jimmy told him about lofty platitudes. Let's examine what occurred.

Mr. Rush:

"I'm sorry to rush you, but if you can take less than the allotted time, I will appreciate it. I have to drive across town later this afternoon. So, what is it?"

Recognizing that he can't make an effective presentation in such a short time, Jimmy opts for a lofty platitude. Mr. Rush is already exhibiting a negative attitude, because he's in a hurry, and his top priority...1. don't make me late...overwhelms everything else. It's intimidation. When Jimmy pricks the lofty platitude with a pin, Mr. Rush responds positively, making the climate more favorable for Jimmy to present his idea properly. It's much like a double negative causing a positive. Further, Jimmy has obtained Mr. Rush's permission for every move he's made.

Jimmy:

"I appreciate that, Mr. Rush, I really do," replied Jimmy. "I can do this in a flash."

What a great word to respond with to a person who is rushing you...'flash'. Jimmy's verbiage and accompanying body language (remaining standing) are testaments that he really will honor Mr. Rush's 'hurry up' request. Sitting down would be aggravating, thus counterproductive.

Jimmy:

"I want to tell you something right now that is really great…so great, in fact, that I can hardly believe it myself!

Even though he says nothing at this point, Mr. Rush probably has negative thoughts.

Mr. Rush's Thoughts:

"These salespeople are all the same. There hasn't been anything great in the grocery business since the invention of the aluminum can."

Jimmy:

"The problem is that I have to use some lofty platitudes to explain it to you…because it really is great…and lofty platitudes usually create negative responses.

Mr. Rush's Thoughts:

"What? I've never heard this before. I don't want any salesperson to believe I've prejudged his product. I'm not negative. I'm a professional buyer. This sounds kind of interesting."

Jimmy:

"And I don't want to go to all the trouble to tell you all about my wonderful idea if you're going to have a negative response."

Mr. Rush:

"What is it?"

His first acquiescence, giving permission to proceed.

Jimmy:

"I've got it right here in my briefcase."

Jimmy knows he's walking on eggs. He needs to continue obtaining permission for everything he does.

Mr. Rush:

"Show me."

Jimmy:

"Do you mind if set my case on your desk?"

If Mr. Rush is late, it's because he gave Jimmy permission to cause him to be late. Allowing Jimmy to proceed causes Mr. Rush to realize he wants to see and hear the idea. He's reaching out for the string.

Mr. Rush:

"Let me move these papers."

In less than a minute, Mr. Rush has discovered that he wants to find out about Jimmy's idea, and that that is more important than 'hurrying Jimmy up.' Besides, maybe one or more of his next appointments will be 'no-shows'. He'll make it across town on time somehow, but not at Jimmy's expense.

We're all deluged by lofty platitudes in our busy lives. Even though Jimmy used one to his advantage with Mr. Rush, in the following situation he must undo the effects of a lofty platitude used on him to his disadvantage.

* * *

The Lofty Introduction

The meeting was about to begin and everyone was there including Jimmy Dover, the guest speaker. The company president asked Billy Bologne, the marketing vice president, to introduce Jimmy to the group. Attending were the treasurer, executive vice president, national sales manager, production manager, and the director of long-range planning. Other members of the company management team were also present, and Jimmy realized that the subject for his talk would probably step on all their toes.

Billy Bologne stood at the head of the conference table and tapped his glass. "We might as well begin," he said. "Jimmy Dover has come a long way, and we're all eager to hear what he has to say. His reputation as a miracle worker precedes him."

Like owls in a treetop, the heads surrounding the table turned to stare at Jimmy. Word had leaked out before the meeting that some superman guy was coming in to shake up the operation. The rumor around the top floor was that Jimmy Dover waved his magic wand, and presto! Production improved, sales soared, marketing problems dissolved, solutions appeared, customer relations improved, and employee morale got a big lift. Billy Bologne did nothing to dispel the rumors in his introductory remarks.

"Jimmy is going to show us how to pare our expenses, dramatically increase our sales, and boost our bottom line. Isn't that right, Jimmy?"

Billy looked at Jimmy and smiled.

"Anyway," said Billy, "I don't want to steal any of his thunder, so let me present our special guest, Mr. Jimmy Dover."

If Jimmy could have put together a national contest to see who could come up with the worst-ever introduction, this would be the prize-winner. Jimmy had not even begun, yet everyone at the meeting had a reason to be offended. He strode to the head of the table.

"Thanks, Bill, for that flowery introduction, but I want to say before I get started that it was a gross overstatement. A gross overstatement. If I, all by myself, could do all of those things, I'd hire out as a million-dollar-a-day consultant, and never need to leave my office. No, it takes much more than that. It's a team effort. The end result of all your efforts as a team is the bottom line and it's the expertise of each manager that makes it happen. Finance, marketing, production, sales, planning…all of those things working in tandem will defy gravity, cause success to jump off the chart, and make the stockholders delirious with joy. What I want to talk about today is very exciting because not only is it a possibility, it is a probability, but only you will decide. And you. And you. And you. And you.

"I have a proposition here, but if it has any merit, it will be obvious within the next two hours. Extremely obvious. But if it doesn't, I'll appreciate it if one of you will stand up and say, 'We work here Jimmy, you don't. We know what will work here, you don't. That will not work here.' At that point I will turn the meeting back to Billy Bologne and leave."

Bologne's introductory assertion that Jimmy was a miracle worker who'd pare expenses, dramatically increase sales and boost the bottom line was recognized by everyone at the meeting as hyperbole. Whopper claims by anyone can cause total disbelief. Every person in the group could ask himself, "How can anyone be that good?" Plus, when the lofty platitude touches an individual's department where the possibility exists that someone else can do better, it could be total tune-out time.

Here are some negative thoughts possibly experienced by those in attendance:

Treasurer:

"What's he talking about? I've already done everything humanly possible to pare our expenses."

National Sales Manager:

"Any plan he has to dramatically improve our sales will be like pulling an elephant through a pool of hardening rubber. It's probably witchcraft."

Production Manager:

"What does he mean, pare the expenses? Don't they know about my plan to retool the plant? What's going on here?"

Director of Long-Range Planning:

"Nobody consulted me about this Dover creep. I thought I was in charge of planning."

Executive VP:

"This will be very interesting."

President:

"No comment."

When Jimmy stood up to address them after Bologne's introduction, he immediately dealt with the situation.

Jimmy:

"Thanks, Bill, for that flowery introduction, but I want to say before I get started that it was a gross overstatement. A gross overstatement."

Jimmy knew he must prick the lofty platitude with a pin to let them know he wasn't a threat to them. Nor did he intend to be.

Jimmy:

"If I, all by myself, could do all of those things, I'd hire out as a million-dollar-a-day consultant and never need to leave my office."

Jimmy plays down his own importance and sets the stage to emphasize theirs.

Jimmy:

"No, it takes much more than that. It's a team effort. The end result of all your efforts as a team is the bottom line and it is the expertise of each manager that makes it happen. Finance, marketing, production, sales, planning…all of those things working in tandem will defy gravity, cause success to jump off the chart, and make the stockholders delirious with joy."

Jimmy includes them all in one sentence, implying he's not important, they are; his plan is not the key, their execution is; his contribution is minimal, their expertise is a necessity; and any resulting benefits will be theirs to enjoy and get credit for.

Jimmy:

"What I want to talk about today is very exciting because not only is it a possibility, it is a probability…"

He uses a mild platitude. Their attitudes are changing. They see Jimmy not as a pompous, stuffed shirt; but as one who acknowledges their importance. Here are some of their possible thoughts.

Treasurer:

"If this plan is any good, they'll probably look at me to come up with the money. Good thing I've got my sandbag fund. The chief will love me."

National Sales Manager:

"He sounds pretty certain about this. Why didn't I bring my tape recorder? Maybe I can use his technique at my next sales meeting."

Production Manager:

"I wonder if it's a new product. It could mean a whole new plant."

Director of Long Range Planning:

"If this gets approved, I'm going to have to know this stuff. I'd better listen and take notes."

Executive VP:

"I wish he'd been with me last week in San Francisco."

President:

"Good move."

Jimmy:

"But only you will decide. And you. And you. And you. And you. I have a proposition here, and if it has any merit, it will be obvious within the next two hours. Extremely obvious. And if it doesn't, I'll appreciate it very much if one of you will stand up and say, 'We work here Jimmy, you don't. We know what will work here, you don't. That will not work here.' At that point I'll turn the meeting back to Billy Bologne and leave."

Jimmy sets up a scenario that he knows cannot occur. It will not be practical for anyone in the room to actually do what he's suggesting, because the chief is present. Only he can invite Jimmy to leave. His non-interference makes it appear that Jimmy has his tacit approval for the entire soon-to-be-heard proposal.

This is also a strong opening for Jimmy's presentation. He has turned the lofty platitude introduction to his advantage by pricking it with a pin by referring to it as a gross overstatement. He has then given everyone credit for being an important part of any decision that will be made and then concludes with a Guts to Fail ending that Pulls the String away from them before they even know what it is. Any initial negative responses have undergone a one hundred eighty degree turnabout, which can be translated in everyone's mind as, "Wow! This must be one fantastic proposition. I'd better listen up!"

Consider how Jimmy would have fared had he not known to Avoid the Lofty Platitude and instead agreed with Billy Bologne?

Jimmy:

"Billy is right, gentlemen. I am a worker of miracles, and my proposition today will pare your expenses, dramatically increase your sales well above your present objectives, and boost your bottom line."

Lofty platitudes are deadly because they cause negative responses. Be careful with them. When you speak and accidentally begin to utter one, you can stop in mid-sentence and start over. They're everywhere…advertising, conversations, written reports, sports broadcasts, correspondence, skywriting, even on tombstones. It takes practice to avoid using them.

By the way, what are you thinking of?

Chapter Four

FBI Interrogation School Questions

No prospect will ever appear with a biography pinned to his jacket, but most salespeople wished they would, because many prospects are reluctant to impart personal information about themselves before they match up with the salesperson. This makes customer-sense, because the prospect does not expect to like the salesperson, but instead is dreading the experience. Thus, the prospect's plan is to get information and give none. Sounds like an impasse, doesn't it? Enter the need for FBI Interrogation School Questions.

Their purpose is to attain information such as the prospect's name, employment status, one or more incomes, other family members, schools attended, residence, own or rent, present vehicles, and more;...a huge challenge in the sales process.

Question. If prospect information is so important, why do so many salespeople not obtain it before selecting a product to present? The answers are several: They're afraid. They don't know how. No one has shown them. The prospect is unresponsive. The prospect controls the situation. Let's examine a typical no-information situation that occurs at a automobile dealership. This chapter is excerpted from the author's book entitled, NonConfrontation Selling...The One-on-One Revolution.

A well-dressed prospect walks toward a lineup of pickups at an automobile dealership, and a salesperson approaches.

"I want to take a look at a pickup," says the prospect.

"This one's our best seller," responds the salesperson. "How do you like it?"

"How much is it?"

"Would you like to go inside and see what we can work out? I know we can save you a lot of money."

"How much?"

Incredibly, situations like this occur. Mr. No Name Salesperson prattling with Mr. No Name Prospect. Afterward, the salesperson learns the prospect is a dishwasher at the local fast-food drive-in, his wife attends school, they and their two toddlers live with her parents, and their present vehicle is fifteen years old. Will the reader agree that the chances for selling this prospect a brand-new truck is about zero? In the above dialogue, though, the salesperson has caused price-dickering on an unattainable vehicle. Even if they go inside to "work something out," both will discover they've been wasting their time, and the prospect will depart without buying anything.

Incidentally, this prospect will purchase a vehicle somewhere within the next few days, and he'll be seen driving around in his newly-acquired, five year old pickup. But Mr. No Name Salesperson won't benefit, nor will the dealership he works for. Reverse situations occur, too, involving prospects with great wealth who dress down for the occasion and wear their grubbies. Some salespeople assume they're poor and either won't greet them at all or will show them too old of a vehicle and offend them. Even someone who's just won the state lottery is smart enough to know not to inform the salesperson of his available cash and good fortune, because by acting poor, he believes he can negotiate the price down.

"How much available cash do you have?" asks the salesperson.

"Not very much," replies the lottery winner.

Obtaining good information about a prospect is not the result of asking direct questions, but instead is the result of properly formulated FBI Interrogation School Questions. Let's take a quick peek at an incorrect FBI interrogation and discover why direct questions are inadequate. The prime suspect for a bank robbery, kidnapping, and murder sat at a long table facing the Inspector and the Chief in the Federal Building downtown.

"Did you do it?" asked the Inspector.

"No, I'm innocent," answered the suspect.

"He didn't do it," said the Inspector to the Chief.

"How do you know that?" asked the Chief.

"He said he didn't," responded the Inspector.

"Well, go ahead and release him then," said the Chief.

Is asking direct questions how the FBI solves a case? Then believing the suspect's replies? Of course not. Direct questions are not the proper way to obtain information. Wary folks withhold. The goal is to cause the prospect to want to volunteer personal information about himself and his family which will evolve into a two-sided dialogue instead of a one-sided monologue. A typical response to an FBI Interrogation School Question is one that goes way beyond the scope of the question and contains unasked for, volunteered information. As dialogue occurs, the salesperson must keep the flow of information going by asking questions about the prospects answers.

* * *

The Seven Most Wanted

FBI Question #1—

"Did you have a long drive getting here today, or do you live close by?"

Sounds innocuous, doesn't it? But it's potent. The first characteristic to observe is that it's literally impossible to answer with one syllable. The prospect must articulate a complete sentence containing a subject and a predicate. One of the goals is to cause the prospect to talk in complete sentences which leads to compound/complex sentences which lead to paragraphs, dialogue and conversation. A typical response is, "Oh, about twenty minutes. We live over by the foothills on the North side."

The second characteristic, in this example, is that the response includes two complete sentences. Third, the prospect volunteers information that is not requested. The FBI question asks only about 'long drive', and the response volunteers a general location..."by the foothills on the North Side." Fourth, the purpose of the question is not obvious. Discovering where he lives is the purpose, but that wasn't specifically asked. Fifth, the question deals with the 'known' instead of the 'unknown'. The prospect is being asked about his most recent experience before he arrived at the store...his drive there. It's true that he could have taken the bus, cab, or trolley, but that's not likely; hence, the first FBI question is about a subject that the prospect knows.

If the question instead had been, "What are you looking for today?" (since the prospect hadn't found it yet) it would have become easy for him to begin a pattern of rejection by responding with, "I don't know. I'm just looking."

The verbiage of a properly formulated FBI Interrogation School Question is critical, every word must be used, or it won't work. Let's read why.

"Did you have a long drive getting here today?"

"No."

Did the prospect reply with a complete sentence containing a subject and a predicate? No, because the salesperson omitted half of the FBI question. The reader can wonder if it's better to cause the prospect to talk in complete sentences and commence a dialogue or to cause him to shrug, grunt, and become monosyllabic?

The gorilla at the zoo can do that.

Which way is more likely to lead to a dialogue and flow of information? There are no shortcuts for FBI Interrogation School Questions. It's all or nothing. Read the question aloud. "Did you have a long drive getting here today, or do you live close by?" When the prospect responds, the salesperson continues the flow by asking a question about the answer.

"Did you have a long drive getting here today, or do you live close by?" asks the salesperson.

"Oh, about twenty minutes," replies the prospect. "We live over by the foothills on the North side."

"Gosh, there's been quite a bit of new development and new construction in that area during the past three or four years, hasn't there?"

"Quite a bit, actually. We live in Brentwood Estates, and we like it pretty well."

"Brentwood Estates. That's nice. Aren't are some really nice homes, condos, and even apartments over in that area?"

"Yes. Ours is a home near the creek."

"Were you one of the first to live in that area?"

"Yes. We've lived there for almost four years now."

"When you say 'we', does that mean there are others in your family?"

The 'flow' continues because the salesperson asks questions about the prospect's answers, although, he's asked only one FBI Interrogation School Question so far. The prospect volunteers more information than requested, and he's responding with complete sentences, some compound sentences; and the result is a dialogue.

It's easy for the prospect, because he's talking about subjects he's familiar with.

Alternately, if the salesperson asked, "What are you looking for?" the prospect would have to talk about a subject he's not familiar with, because he hasn't seen what he's looking for yet, and the chance for a dialogue becomes more difficult.

Consider the amount of information the salesperson has about the prospect. He knows where he lives, an upscale subdivision nearby, that he owns a home in Brentwood by the creek, that he's lived there with his family for almost four years. Isn't this data helpful to the salesperson to determine the prospect's standard-of-living, lifestyle, income bracket? If the salesperson didn't practice the discipline about asking questions about the answers, he may have learned only that the prospect lives in Brentwood Estates, but not that he owns. Some people reside with friends, parents, co-workers, or rent...any number of cogent possibilities.

The salesperson has proceeded from the general to the specific. The FBI Interrogation School Question opens a general subject, and the reward for asking questions about answers causes the information to proceed from the general to the specific.

Let's digress for a moment to illustrate an inferior method that obtains some information, but develops no rapport, dialogue, or volunteered information.

"Where do you live?" asks the salesperson.

"Brentwood" replies the prospect.

"Been there long?"

"Yes."

"Married?

"Yes."

Question. Does the salesperson seem interested in any of the prospect's replies? No. How can he seem interested when he changes the subject after every monosyllabic response. Another question. Are the prospect's replies conversational? Only if you enjoy talking to the elevator voice. Read how few words the salesperson uses in his questions. The prospect follows suit. He's more likely to answer with complete sentences after the salesperson asks questions in complete sentences. More detail.

"Did you have a long drive getting here today, or do you live close by?" asks the salesperson.

"It took us about a half hour or so," replies the prospect.

"A half hour or so? What's a half hour from here?"

"We live out by Willetsville on Route 26."

"Willetsville. Gosh, that's pretty nice out there. There's been some new construction and development out in that area, hasn't there, over the past three or four years?

"Not too much, thank goodness. We have a farm house out there."

"Well, when you drive back there from here, are you on this side of Willetsville or over on the other side?"

"Our place is just before you get to the city limits."

"If you drive back on Route 26, what's the major crossroad just before your farm?"

"Thompson Road. In fact, that's where we turn off."

The prospect is giving the salesperson a verbal road map to his house. Was that his plan before he arrived at the dealership? Of course not. Yet, the salesperson obtains this information without confrontation simply by asking questions about the prospect's answers, and in the process he exhibits strong interest in what he is hearing. Will this increase the odds that the prospect may become more interested in the salesperson. Of course. There's another ingredient, which is included in the following dialogue. Make a statement about the answer before asking a question about the answer.

The salesperson replies. "Thompson Road. Oh sure. I pass there every time I drive out that way. Let me ask you, when you said 'we', in reference to where you live, does that mean it's not just you in your family?"

"Sure. My wife, and we have two girls," says the prospect

"Two girls. I have two girls, replies the salesperson. "And three boys. The way we worked it out was boy-girl-boy-girl-boy. They're still talking about it at the doctor's office. How old is your oldest?"

"Eight. And the youngest is six."

"What's your oldest's name?"

"Jessica."

"She must be in what, the third grade now?"

"Yes. She attends Willetsville Elementary."

"What about your youngest? What's her name?"

"Elie. She's in the first grade."

"Nice ages. Great names.

* * *

FBI Question #2—

"Is one of the reasons why you live in that area because it is close to where you work?"

Discovering his employment is this question's goal, but its purpose is not obvious, because it's linked to a subject that's already being discussed…where they live. The questioner uses the 'known' to discover the 'unknown'. The question follows so closely in the dialogue about where the prospect lives that it seems a natural continuation of that subject. Exact wording is vital. The word "one" is utterly important. Don't omit it. Why? The prospect is more likely to respond conversationally. Eliminate "one", and the wording becomes "Is the reason why…" and the meaning changes to either it's the most important reason or is the only reason. But including "one" connotes that it may be one of many reasons, thus the odds increase for a dialogue and decrease for a one syllable reply. Returning to the prospect from Willetsville, let's continue with the second FBI Interrogation School Question.

"Is one of the reasons why you folks live in that area because it is close to where you work?" asks the salesperson.

"It takes about forty five minutes," answers the prospect. "I'm the district manager for Banana Computers downtown in the Tower Building."

"Banana Computers? What a big company. When you say you're the district manager, does that mean you're in charge of the entire department?"

"Yes, the marketing division. I oversee ten branch offices in a three state area."

"What a big responsibility. Does that mean you have to travel a lot in your job?"

"Sure does, but my overnights average about two per week."

"Sounds like you really like it."

"It's challenging."

"Have you been with them for quite some time?"

"Ten years now."

"I've always wondered about that. When you retire from a company like Banana Computers, do you get a gold-plated mouse?"

"That's pretty good. I'll have to tell that to my boss."

One reason why this dialogue produces so much information is because the salesperson asks questions about the prospect's answers, and the result is a showing of great interest. If the prospect suspects that the salesperson's interest is not genuine , he'll clam up and become non-responsive. Same if the salesperson expresses no interest at all. Reread the foregoing dialogue.

Doesn't the salesperson appear vitally interested in the prospect and where he works? Isn't he indicating that the prospect's work is important and that he's impressed with the prospect's success? Will the information that was volunteered assist the salesperson to determine how expensive of a vehicle the prospect can afford?

The salesperson could simply have asked him where he works, but would the answer, "Banana Computers," have been adequate? The janitor works there. The top-producing salesperson works there. The night watchman works there. The part-time office clerk works there. Their incomes are disparate. But, by first asking the FBI question to introduce the general topic, then asking questions about the answers and going from the general to the specific, the salesperson develops a good dialogue and information flow that is vital to the forward movement of the sales process.

If a prospect indicates that he's retired, the question 'retired from what?' should pop in one's mind. Bums are retired. Three star admirals are retired. There's a vast difference in their retirement pay. It's easy to realize that general information is not good enough when qualifying a prospect, so moving from the general to the specific is highly appropriate.

* * *

FBI Question #3—

(To spouse) "Do you work outside the home?"

Watch a woman get riled by asking her, "Do you work?" Fire and brimstone commences, or at least an icy coolness that results in no sale. Of course the woman works. If she's a homemaker, she works twenty-four hours per day. The three word question, "Do you work?", implies that the role of the homemaker is not work. Instead ask, "Do you work outside the home?", and the inference becomes "Do you have two jobs?" That becomes a compliment to her work ethic and the role of a homemaker. Learning whether your prospect's family has two incomes is this question's goal, and like the other FBI questions, its purpose is not obvious. Two incomes can qualify more easily for an expensive new or used vehicle easier than one. If the answer is 'yes', then ask questions about the answers to learn what the specific job is in order to determine her approximate income.

* * *

FBI Question #4—

"Are you looking for a vehicle similar to the one you are presently driving?"

The first product question. There's much to examine here. The prospect is very familiar with his present vehicle and can talk knowledgeably about it, thus this question is an excellent example of 'talking about the known to discover the unknown'. Savvy shoppers have a mantra they use when they wish to be left alone in a retail establishment..."I'm just looking." Notice that 'looking' is the third word in the FBI question. The salesperson's usage of that word makes it difficult for the prospect to use afterward as a shun.

"Are you looking for a vehicle similar to the one you are presently driving?" asks the salesperson.

The prospect replies, "No, I'm just looking."

Ridiculous, isn't it? The prospect is required to slow down and create an original rejoinder. As a result, he answers the FBI question directly. Let's start it again.

"Are you looking for a vehicle similar to the one you are presently driving?" asks the salesperson.

"No, I'm looking for something a little bigger," replies the prospect.

"What kind of vehicle are you presently driving?"

"A Honda Civic."

"Wow. You have a Honda Civic? What year is it?"

"It's three years old."

"Is three years how long you've owned it?"

"Yes. I bought it new."

"Is your Civic a two-door or a four-door?"

"It's a two-door."

"So, when you say you're looking for something a little bigger, are you looking for something bigger in a two-door or a four-door?"

"I think a four-door this time."

"Is one of the reasons why you're looking for something bigger this time because of your family?"

"Yes. With our two kids getting bigger, the Civic is just too small for us."

"If you get another vehicle, who would drive it the most?"

"I would. My wife has her Oldsmobile to drive around in."

The prospect is actually informing the salesperson what he's looking for by describing his present vehicle and the changes he'd like. His description of the 'known' vehicle better enables the salesperson to select the 'unknown' replacement for it.

* * *

Another situation. Same FBI question. The prospect has three possible responses, 1) Bigger; 2) Smaller; 3) Same size.

"Are you looking for a vehicle similar to the one you are presently driving?" asks the salesperson.

"No," replies the prospect. "I'm looking for something quite a bit smaller."

"What kind of vehicle is your present one?"

"It's a Buick Park Avenue, four years old."

"Isn't your Park Avenue a four door?"

'Yes it is."

"Well, when you say you're looking for something quite a bit smaller, are you looking for something smaller in a four-door or in a two-door?"

"Another four-door would be nice."

A picture unfolds describing a vehicle that he's looking for, as the prospect comfortably describes his present vehicle, and the salesperson obtains this vital information before he selects a vehicle to show to this prospect.

* * *

FBI Question #5—

"If you get another vehicle, will that make you a two-car family?"

Discovering whether the prospect is planning to trade in his present vehicle is this question's goal, and like the previous FBI Questions, its purpose is not obvious, but instead sounds like a compliment. "Are you rich?" "Will you have two cars?" It's difficult for a prospect to be put off by a question that implies a compliment. A potential problem posed by asking the prospect directly if he's going to trade in his vehicle is that it implies that he's buying today, and wariness raises its ugly head. Even if it doesn't, the prospect can veer the conversation into "How much can I get for it?" Instead of steering into disaster, the salesperson continues the interview with FBI Question #5.

"If you get another vehicle, will that make you a two-car family?" asks the salesperson.

"I have an old truck at home that I use," replies the prospect, "but I plan to trade in my Buick if I find what I'm looking for."

In this case, the prospect uses the term 'trade-in' first.

* * *

FBI Question #6 -

"When you bought your present vehicle, did you pay cash for it?"

It's the only question that's eliciting a simple 'yes' or 'no', as its purpose is to determine whether the prospect is seeking to finance. Like the previous FBI question, it implies a compliment. "Are you rich?" "Wow, you can afford to pay cash for expensive things." The interview proceeds.

"When you bought your present vehicle, did you pay cash for it?" asks the salesperson.

"No, I financed it," answers the prospect.

* * *

FBI Question #7 -

"On your present vehicle, are there any features that you particularly like that you would like to have again if you replace it with another vehicle? For example, does your present vehicle have a stick shift or automatic?"

A payoff now occurs, as a complete picture of the desired vehicle is described by the prospect. Ironically, he's thinking only of his present vehicle. He's mentally inside his own vehicle. Again, it's the technique of using the known to discover the unknown.

"On your present vehicle," asks the salesperson, "are there any features that you particularly like that you would like to have again if you replace it with another vehicle? For example, does your present vehicle have a stick shift or automatic?"

"We both prefer an automatic," replies the prospect.

"How important is air-conditioning?"

"Very. It gets hot. We'd like to have power seats and power door locks, too.

"You know what? I think I have a couple of good ideas. Follow me."

The salesperson walks ahead of the prospect to the vehicle or vehicles he's opted to show, not vice versa; and he does it after he's obtained the necessary information from the prospect, not before. Everything the salesperson says has a purpose, nothing is idle chitchat. The FBI Interrogation School Questions have an order, and each response from the prospect forms a better picture in the salesperson's mind about the prospect, his family, occupation, lifestyle, and desired vehicle. If the salesperson learns that the prospect lives in a poor neighborhood, has a low income job, then proceeds to show him the top-of-the-line or a new model, of course the prospect will like the vehicle; but the challenge is to select and present not only a vehicle that the prospect will like, but one he can afford to buy. Show a mansion on Nob Hill and ask the client if he likes it. Of course. Who wouldn't? But, can he afford it? If not, can he buy it? No.

* * *

Microwave Store

The owner of a microwave oven store informed the author that he'd been constantly unhappy about his salespeople showing prospects the wrong ovens. His advertising featured loss-leaders. When a respondent to his ads asked, "Is this the model in the ad?" and the salespeople responded, "Yes", and the prospect asked, "Does it do everything?" and the salespeople answered, "It sure does", and the prospect replied, "I think I'll buy it", she took it home and discovered that it didn't; and customer satisfaction plummeted. The store owner requested a list of FBI Interrogation School Questions. Here they are:

1. Are you a gourmet cook?
2. How often during the year do you prepare a dinner as elaborate as one your family used to prepare for Thanksgiving?
3. How often do you entertain at home?

4. Are you so busy sometimes that you simply throw a tv dinner in the oven because you're so tired after work?
5. Are you looking for a microwave oven similar to the one you are presently using?

6. Are there any features on your present microwave oven that you really like that you'd like to have again if you replace it with a new oven?

They worked. His customers who purchased the cheaper ovens were the fast-food junkies, the high-line purchasers were those gourmets, who prepare elaborate meals frequently. But, one doesn't find out if one doesn't find out.

* * *

Singles Bars

Another acquaintance asked if FBI Interrogation School Questions could be utilized in a singles bar. Why not? The writer created a short list, advised the acquaintance to not change a single word, and asked for the results. Less than a week later the happy bachelor reported his findings. Here's a dialogue containing the list.

"Did you girls have a long drive getting here tonight," asked the bachelor, "or do you live close by?"

Felicity looked into his eyes. "About ten minutes," she answered. "We live together in the Broadway Apartments off of 10th."

"How convenient," commented the bachelor. "It's close to town and a pretty nice neighborhood."

"We like it," said Felicity. She smiled.

"Is one of the reasons why you two live there because it is close to where you work? (to Felicity) Let me ask you first."

"I don't," she said, "but Venus does. I work at the First National Bank in Highland Park, but Venus is attending beauty college on Broadway just three blocks from our apartment."

"Does that mean you can walk there, Venus?" inquired the bachelor.

"Yes. Felicity always has the car," purred Venus.

"It sure is nice meeting you two," said the bachelor. "My name is Jason, Jason Argonaut. What is your name?"

"Venus Cauldron. This is my roomie, Felicity Fox."

"Venus Cauldron and Felicity Fox," repeated the bachelor. "Is it just the two of you there?"

"Yes. How about you?" asked Felicity.

"My roommate's meeting me here in fifteen minutes, replied the bachelor. "He works late."

What's his name?" asked Venus.

The reader can recognize the FBI Interrogation School Questions, and appreciate the discipline of asking questions about the answers, progressing from the general to the specific, and asking about the known to discover the unknown. In all endeavors they're useful, practical, and effective, not to mention fun.

* * *

Ironically, a dialogue containing only FBI Interrogation School Questions develops no specific information. Let's read why. The situation includes the salesperson meeting a man and woman, who are together.

"Did you have a long drive getting here today or do you live close by?" asks the salesperson.

"About a hour, I guess," answers the man. "I live over the county line in Brockton.

"Is one of the reasons why you live in that area because it is close to where you work?"

"Yes," answers the man.

The salesperson looks at the woman. "Do you work outside the home?"

"Yes," she says.

"Are you looking for a vehicle similar to the one you are presently driving?" asks the salesperson.

"No," replies the man.

"If you get another vehicle, will that make you a two car family?"

"No," replies the man.

"When you bought your present vehicle," asks the salesperson, "did you pay cash for it?"

"No," replies the man.

"On your present vehicle," asks the salesperson, "are there any features that you particularly like that you would like to have again if you you replace it with another vehicle? For example, does your present vehicle have a stick shift or automatic?"

"It's an automatic," replies the man.

"I've got a couple of ideas," says the salesperson. "Follow me."

What ideas could the salesperson possibly have? He obtained practically no information about the prospects, nor features for a desired vehicle. He doesn't even know if the prospect would prefer an automatic transmission on his next vehicle, only that his present one has one. He doesn't know if they're married. What's he going to show them? Maybe the tooth fairy knows. Properly, the salesperson must ask an FBI Interrogation School Question, get a response, then ask questions about the answers to develop specific information before he asks the next FBI Interrogation School Question. In the preceding dialogue, the salesperson didn't learn where in Brockton the prospect lives. Maybe he has a tent pitched on the creek. Maybe the salesperson assumed he's well-off because of his attire. Maybe he's a valet in a mansion. Maybe the salesperson watched him get out of an expensive vehicle. But what if the vehicle is borrowed or belongs to a friend or relative? The salesperson did not develop information regarding the prospect's employment, only that he works close to Brockton. And even though the spouse informed him that she does indeed work outside the home, where??...what?? And what features on their present vehicle would they like on a replacement vehicle if they get one? Zero information.

* * *

Memorize the seven FBI questions in the most logical order.

1. Did you have a long drive getting here today, or do you live close by?
2. Is one of the reasons why you live in that area because it is close to where you work?
3. (to spouse) Do you work outside the home?
4. Are you looking for a vehicle similar to the one you are presently driving?
5. If you get another vehicle, will that make you a two car family?
6. When you bought your present vehicle, did you pay cash for it?
7. On your present vehicle, are there any particular features that you particularly like that you would like to have again if you replace it with another vehicle? For example, does your present vehicle have a stick shift or automatic?

Now look at the list in total. Observe that the first three questions concern personal information. The last four are product-oriented. Personal information first...product information second.

On the reader's next shopping trip to any retail store observe whether the salesperson he meets talks first about personal or product information. If he asks, "See anything you like?" he flunks. Or "How can I help you today?" Or "The item you're looking at is one of our best sellers." Don't do that. Even the most untalented salesperson can show the wrong product for lack of information, which is bound to occur when he proceeds with inadequate information and false assumptions.

Reread the list of questions again. Is the word 'buy' in any? The word 'bought' is in the sixth question, but it's used in reference to their present vehicle. 'Buy' is a scary word early in the sales process, as prospects get defensive, and it must be absent from FBI Interrogation School Questions. Examples to shun: "Are you buying or looking?" asks the salesperson. "Just looking," responds the prospect. "Nice day to buy a new car, huh?" asks the salesperson. "I'm on my lunch hour," answers the prospect as he looks at his watch. "Can only stay a minute."

A final word on this subject...practice. What are you thinking of?

Chapter Five

Theater of the Mind

The Telephone

What an invention! The telephone in the right hands can work wonders. It's better than television, because we can create our own scenes instead of having them created for us. It encourages creativity, imagination, even artistry.

In the same way a master painter uses the proper colors, shades, brush sizes, strokes, and composition to create a masterpiece, one can use the telephone with the proper words, expressions, nuances, pauses and inflections to create Theater of the Mind.

With the telephone, it's possible to paint a picture of yourself that you could never create on television or in person. Before television came along in the early 1950's, radio was popular for dramatic shows. In the evening after dinner, entire families sat around the radio listening to The Whistler, Amos 'n' Andy, Gangbusters, Our Miss Brooks, and Fibber McGee and Molly. How about The Shadow, Suspense, First Nighter or Dragnet? Action, suspense, mystery, drama, comedy, entertainment. Sam Spade was played by Howard Duff, Mr. Boynton by Jeff Chandler, Miss Brooks by Eve Arden and Matt Dillon by William Conrad, who is better known for his Cannon television series.

Though we couldn't see them, we all thought we knew what the characters looked like, because we carried an image in our mind. All of the action was played out in our imagination. Remember Jack Benny's train announcer who intoned, "Anaheim-Azusa-Cucamonga"? Think of how much more difficult it is to walk on water or part the Red Sea on television than on the radio. Even today, when we listen to a disc jockey on the radio and then finally see him in person, he doesn't look at all the way we imagined. That's because of Theater of the Mind, which does not exist when we watch television. We don't have the opportunity to use our imagination with television, because everything is right there in front of us. And that's a shame! There's a possibility that today's kids, raised on television, will not be as imaginative and inventive as those of previous generations.

We still, however, have the telephone, so fantastic opportunities still exist to develop the high profile sales tactic of Theater of the Mind to its utmost.

Imagination is the key. Cause the person you are phoning to imagine something about you. If you can do this, you'll unlock the secret of walking on water and will begin to master Theater of the Mind.

In the following situation Jimmy has several objectives, but his first hurdle is getting past the switchboard operator who screens all the boss's calls. If Jimmy sounds like just another peddler, the switchboard operator will sidetrack him. So, he leaves a few things to her imagination.

* * *

Disorganizing the Receptionist

Precisely at 6:30 a.m. the ringing phone jarred Jimmy Dover awake. When he'd left a wake-up call with the hotel operator the night before, shortly after arriving from the airport, Jimmy knew it would be a great day, because nobody knew anything, and that was just as he'd planned.

As with most of his sales trips, he knew nobody in the city, nobody knew he was coming, nobody had received any information about him or his company. In effect, the entire city was a blank slate ready to be filled in with sales; and nobody, including Jimmy, had any preconceived notions about his business.

The telephone book lay next to the phone on the lamp table, and Jimmy smiled at it. That and his telephone pitch was all he needed. He knew that by eleven o'clock, he'd have at least ten solid appointments with enthusiastic prospects.

After breakfast at 8:30, Jimmy opened the yellow pages, and dialed the number of the first automobile dealer he saw listed. On this particular trip, Jimmy's objective was to sell an automobile advertising campaign. As the phone rang, Jimmy smiled at the thought that if this dealer were interested, by this afternoon, he'd be signing him up for a campaign about which, at this very moment, he knew nothing.

"Good morning, Blitz Buick," answered the switchboard operator.

Instantly, Jimmy metamorphosed. No longer the confident-sounding person of a moment before, he transformed into an innocent country bumpkin.

"Oh no!" he replied. "You...uh...answered the phone so fast, I forgot what I'm calling about." He paused. "Just a second. Oh, I know. Say, uh, who's the owner there?"

"The owner?" asked the receptionist.

Jimmy knew that she couldn't possibly know whether he was a long-term customer with a flat tire calling from the freeway, a family member, a factory VIP, or what? He strove to not sound like a salesperson. He realized that most of them sounded slick, polished, professional, and that switchboard operators were well-trained to spot them by their demeanor so they could screen them from the boss.

For example, if a sales representative from the local television station made the error of identifying himself as such, the switchboard operator's reply would be, "Oh, you want to speak with Mr. Young, our advertising manager. He's not here today, but if you leave your name and number, I'll see that he gets it." Or, "Would you like to leave a message on his voice mail?"

Of course, all good television time sales representatives should know that it's the owner who buys advertising, not the ad manager. Furthermore, most salespeople know that if their only mission is to provide the advertising manager with their name and number, they can simply mail their business card to him and accomplish that.

Jimmy knew he didn't want to talk to an advertising manager who usually didn't have the authority to buy his program without the owner's permission. He also knew that even if the advertising manager did see the campaign first, he probably wouldn't like it, because it wasn't his own idea. Never take a no from someone who isn't authorized to say yes. Jimmy recalled those words of wisdom from time to time and adhered to the thought. He couldn't remember whether they emanated from Plato or Calvin Coolidge or someone else, but it didn't matter.

He held onto the phone and answered. "Uh, yes, that's it, who is the owner there?"

"That would be Mr. Blatz."

"Then, that's who I guess I want to talk to. Is he in right now?"

"One moment, please."

Usually, it was that simple. Jimmy sounded like someone he wasn't, and the receptionist wasn't preprogrammed to screen this kind of individual from the owner. There are numerous variations to this approach, and Jimmy knows most of them.

Let's go back ten seconds in the dialogue and read how things would have developed if the switchboard operator had been tougher.

Jimmy asked, "Is he in right now?"

"Whom may I say is calling?"

"I'm Jimmy Dover."

"What is this in regard to?"

"What?"

"What is this in regard to?"

"What is what in regard to?"

"Whom are you with?"

"I'm not with anybody. I'm all by myself. I'm the Lone Ranger."

"One moment please."

Preprogrammed switchboard operators can go just so far, particularly in a busy office. Besides, if a crazy person calls, they're more likely to let the boss take care of him. Some companies get so many incoming calls that even the best-trained switchboard operator can't take more than five to ten seconds with each one. The foregoing took one-half minute. And, now Jimmy was next to talk with the chief. He'd never met him, they weren't college chums, no mutual friend arranged an introduction. But, Jimmy was prepared. He knew how to use the telephone to develop Theater of the Mind.

* * *

When the Chief Answers, Turn Into Columbo

Jimmy heard the receiver being picked up at the other end.

The voice said, "George Blatz here."

Jimmy replied with a lilting uplift in his voice...almost a tone of amazement. "Is this Mr. Blatz?"

"Yes." His tone was friendly. For all he knew, the caller might be ordering a fleet of Buicks.

Notice that Jimmy asks, "Is this Mr. Blatz?" instead of, "Are you Mr. Blatz?" The latter is always used by a policeman or teacher, any authority figure. Jimmy couldn't represent authority at this point. That would ruin it. He must be the exact opposite, the humble inquirer. It would be different when and if Jimmy meets Mr. Blatz in person for the first time. Then, Jimmy could appear to be in awe of him, and when shaking his hand, Jimmy could say with awe, "Are you Mr. Blatz?" His eyes would widen with admiration. The general impression would be, "Are you the Great Mr. Blatz? Wow! I've finally met the Great Mr. Blatz! I'm never going to wash this hand again!" And Mr. Blatz might react by thinking, "This very perceptive and intelligent man thinks I am big and important. I can hardly wait to look in the mirror."

Jimmy gripped the phone as he sat in his hotel room. "Mr. Blatz, I'm Jimmy Dover, from the West Coast? First, I probably have a little bad news. I'm not calling to buy a fleet of Buicks or anything like that."

"Oh no. That's too bad!"

"Yes, I know it is, and I really don't like to tell you that. Actually, Mr. Blatz, I'm in the advertising business, and I work with about two hundred or so car dealers all over the country and even in Canada and Australia. But I always say, in a hundred years or so, what difference will it make? Two hundred years, anyway."

Mr. Blatz remained silent.

Jimmy hadn't told him anything about his advertising yet, only that he wasn't buying a fleet of Buicks and that in two hundred years from now it might not matter that he's doing business all over the country and in Canada and Australia. Jimmy was getting Mr. Blatz's imagination working.

Jimmy continued. "My company has developed a complete advertising program for automobile dealers, Mr. Blatz. You know, for use in the newspaper and radio...even television. And, yes, I know, you could paint your name on a rock and roll it out onto the street and I suppose that would be advertising, but this is built around something very appealing...the good old days, the Roaring Twenties, complete with barbershop quartets, jazz bands, even an impression of Ted Lewis and Al Jolson, You know? The vaudeville guys? You're probably not ready for this, Mr. Blatz, but it would come across like..Blatz Buick, That Magnificent Man and His Driving Machines. That's the theme! And you could have sales events like The Great Race, The Magnificent Driving Machine Marathon, The Roaring Twenties Sale; it's endless! In any event, Mr. Blatz, the reason I'm trying to track you down is I want to see if I can interest you taking a look at my program while I'm in the area for the next couple of days or so?"

After a moment of silence, Blatz replied. "Well, I'm always willing to take a look. But I can't promise anything."

"Of course not, Mr. Blatz. Of course not. And, I could work myself around any schedule you might have. I could toddle over there this afternoon sometime, say right after three o'clock or so, if, well, if that sounds okay."

"That would be all right. Maybe I'll arrange to have my general manager there, too."

"That would be just great, Mr. Blatz. Will I get lost or anything finding my way to your place?"

Blatz proceeded to give explicit directions. Jimmy already knew the way; but he also knew that Blatz might wonder afterward why he was so anxious for Jimmy not to get lost. Blatz might realize that he had a tremendous desire to see Jimmy's program and to meet Jimmy in person; and this process of wondering whether Jimmy would actually find the place would make his own interest clearer to Blatz.

"Well, thanks a lot, Mr. Blatz," said Jimmy. "I'm pretty sure I'll be there between three and three fifteen, though those big freeways scare me to death. But don't worry. Anyway, why don't you go ahead and carve my name on your desk. It's Jimmy Dover. Jimmy Dover."

"I've got it. Used a machete."

"Great! Great! Well, I guess I'll see you then around three or so if I don't get lost, and I promise you, Mr. Blatz, you'll know in ten minutes if you don't like my program. And if you don't, don't worry, that's okay, because I always find a home for my program before I leave town."

"Okay, Jimmy. See you this afternoon. I'll be glad to pick you up if you like?"

"Thanks, Mr. Blatz. I really appreciate that. But, that's okay. If I get lost, I'll stop at a gas station or something. So, I'll just plan to see you then. Don't forget."

"I won't forget."

Jimmy's use of Theater of the Mind has allowed him to get inside Mr. Blatz's mind, walk around and become irresistible. And, this was all accomplished on the telephone...out of the blue. If someone were to ask Mr. Blatz to try not think of Jimmy Dover, would his brain be occupied by a big, delicious orange?

Let's examine the foregoing more closely.

* * *

Mr. Blatz:

"George Blatz here."

Jimmy:

"Is this Mr. Blatz?"

Jimmy never addresses a person he's just meeting by his first name. Even though many believe this is old-fashioned, the author submits that people desire and admire respect. How can they be offended by it? But, over-familiarity too soon sometimes causes disrespect.

Mr. Blatz:

"Yes."

He is friendly, as he doesn't know the caller or why he's calling. Customers ofttimes get better treatment on the phone than anonymous callers.

Jimmy:

"Mr. Blatz, I'm Jimmy Dover, from the West Coast?"

Mr. Blatz thinks Jimmy is calling long distance, even though Jimmy hasn't said so, and there's a possibility that Mr. Blatz may also believe he should have heard of Jimmy before, because Jimmy put a question mark after his name and location. On the other hand, Jimmy did not mention the name of his company. If he'd said, "I'm Jimmy Dover from XYZ Corporation," there is a high probability that Mr. Blatz would have replied, "I've never heard of you." Even if he only thinks it, it's just as damaging to the forward progress of the dialogue.

Jimmy:

"First, I probably have a little bad news. I'm not calling to buy a fleet of Buicks or anything like that."

Mr. Blatz:

"Oh no. That's too bad!"

Jimmy's is an excellent opening statement, because it almost always receives a friendly, jovial response. Let's digress for a moment and look at another example.

*　　　*　　　*

A woman phones you at home and says, "Is this the Smith residence?

You answer, "Yes."

She replies, "Oh wonderful. At last! I'm Lana Lanna, with the YMCA? First, I probably have a little bad news. I'm not calling to tell you that you and your family are going to receive free memberships in the YMCA for a whole year."

And you reply, "Oh no! That's too bad."

"Yes, I know," she answers. "But family activities are truly a wonderful way for families to share. I mean, of course, the family activities at the YMCA."

"Of course."

"But, it's not all bad. You and your family still have a really wonderful opportunity to participate in "Y" programs, because the kids will all get a free membership when Mom and Dad join for a year..."

This example shows how the caller loosens up Smith with the bad news, then gets him to accept the basic premise of the pitch...the usefulness of a family membership. Let's return to Jimmy and Mr. Blatz.

* * *

If Jimmy had begun with, "Hello, Mr. Blatz, I'm Jimmy Dover with XYZ Corporation. We're an advertising agency," there's the probability that Mr. Blatz would have answered with, "I never heard of you. Besides our advertising needs are well taken care of right now. But, thanks for calling." And Jimmy's call would be terminated before he got started.

Jimmy:

"Yes, I know it is, and I really don't like to tell you that. Actually, Mr. Blatz, I'm in the advertising business, and I work with about two hundred or so car dealers all over the country and even in Canada and Australia. But I always say, in a hundred years or so, what difference will it make? Two hundred years, anyway."

Mr. Blatz could inform Jimmy that he's not interested, but Jimmy's information regarding his working with a wide range of dealers is a lot not be interested in. Besides, he's a world traveler, doesn't mind poking fun at himself, and has a disarming approach. And mystifyingly, how did he get past the careful screening of his well-trained switchboard operator?

In the next monologue, Jimmy informs Mr. Blatz fourteen specific reasons why he might be interested in the campaign...and each contains few words and are offered like machine gun bullets. Notice, too, that Jimmy doesn't treat a possible turndown as a win or lose situation.

Jimmy:

"My company has developed a complete advertising program for automobile dealers, Mr. Blatz. You know, for use in the newspaper and radio...even television. And, yes, I know, you could paint your name on a rock and roll it out onto the street and I suppose that would be advertising, but this is built around something very appealing...the good old days, the Roaring Twenties, complete with barbershop quartets, jazz bands, even an impression of Ted Lewis and Al Jolson, You know? The vaudeville guys? You're probably not ready for this, Mr. Blatz, but it would come across like..Blatz Buick, That Magnificent Man and His Driving Machines. That's the theme! And you could have sales events like The Great Race, The Magnificent Driving Machine Marathon, The Roaring Twenties Sale; it's endless! In any event, Mr. Blatz, the reason I'm trying to track you down is I want to see if I can interest you taking a look at my program while I'm in the area for the next couple of days or so?"

If Mr. Blatz says no, he knows he'll never see or hear from Jimmy again. The last thirteen words finally let him know that Jimmy is not calling long distance. Jimmy has made it easy for him to say no. He's not asking Mr. Blatz to buy or even to like the program, he only inquires whether he'd like to take a look at it. Allowing Mr. Blatz's imagination, Theater of the Mind, to go to work, Jimmy has created a mental picture of himself that Mr. Blatz likes. Jimmy is not the typical vendor asking for an order prematurely...he's different somehow. Concurrently, Jimmy was weaving Theater of the Mind into some of his program's highlights. That's a lot for Mr. Blatz to say no to...if any part of it has piqued his interest.

Mr. Blatz:

"Well, I'm always willing to take a look. But I can't promise anything."

Jimmy:

"Of course not, Mr. Blatz. Of course not."

Mr. Blatz is turned on by one or more of the fourteen bullets. Jimmy doesn't know which ones, but now is not the time to ask.

Many salespeople, though, use the phone and keep their mission a dark secret. They utter lofty platitudes like, "I've got a great advertising program that will substantially increase your sales and save you a lot of money." Even if the prospect asks what it is, the salesperson feigns mystery by saying, "I can't explain it over the phone, but it will certainly be worth your time; and you'll be doing yourself a great service if you meet with me."

Ofttimes, the prospect rings off, thinking, "Another oversold-on-his-own-product salesperson who will waste my time. Every salesperson believes his product or service is the greatest thing since the aluminum can."

Jimmy:

"And, I could work myself around any schedule you might have. I could toddle over there this afternoon sometime, say right after three o'clock or so, if, well, if that sounds okay."

Jimmy is suggesting an available time, but he also sounds accommodating, vulnerable, likable; and he causes Mr. Blatz to feel as though he (Blatz) is in control. The proper choice of words is important in creating Theater of the Mind. After all, do high pressure salespeople "toddle over?"

Mr. Blatz:

"That would be all right. Maybe I'll arrange to have my general manager there, too."

A strong buying signal. Although the word 'buying' is not exactly appropriate. 'Personal acceptance' should be substituted. Mr. Blatz likes one or more of the fourteen benefits so, he wants at least two people at his company to take the time to look at Jimmy's campaign. He's putting together a buying situation. Two things occur in tandem. The prospect likes Jimmy...and he likes something about the campaign. If he didn't, it's unlikely he'd agree to a meeting, regardless of how attractive the program might sound. Salespeople who have difficulty making appointments...even though they have an outstanding product or service...are unsuccessful because they're not making a tandem presentation. You must sell yourself concurrently.

Jimmy:

"That would be just great, Mr. Blatz. Will I get lost or anything finding my way to your place?"

Here, Jimmy asks Mr. Blatz to sell him something, because Jimmy recognizes that this will cause Mr. Blatz to know he wants to like Jimmy's campaign. Otherwise, why would the prospect be trying to selling the seller something? What Mr. Blatz is sell is how easy it is to get to his office.

Jimmy:

(After Mr. Blatz gives him directions) "Well, thanks a lot, Mr. Blatz. "I'm pretty sure I'll be there between three and three fifteen, though those big freeways scare me to death. But don't worry. Anyway, why don't you go ahead and carve my name on your desk. It's Jimmy Dover. Jimmy Dover."

Mr. Blatz:

"I've got it. Used a machete."

Jimmy:

"Great! Great! Well, I guess I'll see you then around three or so if I don't get lost, and I promise you, Mr. Blatz, you'll know in ten minutes if you don't like my program. And if you don't, don't worry, that's okay, because I have a lot of other appointments, and I always find a home for my program before I leave town."

Jimmy doesn't let up about getting lost, and he introduces the strong point that he has only one campaign to sell. This point is not lost on Mr. Blatz, whose next comment is a plea for Jimmy not to get lost.

Mr. Blatz:

"Okay, Jimmy. See you this afternoon. I'll be glad to pick you up if you like?"

Mr. Blatz has just made his first concession by showing his eagerness to see the campaign right away.

Jimmy:

"Thanks, Mr. Blatz. I really appreciate that. But, that's okay. If I get lost, I'll stop at a gas station or something. So, I'll just plan to see you then. Don't forget."

Mr. Blatz:

"I won't forget."

He won't either. In fact, he'll probably talk to his general manager about the unusual phone call, and the general manager will discern that the boss is already interested, so he'll be very attentive at the meeting rather than patronizing. In the meantime, Mr. Blatz will be feeling emotions he usually doesn't. Why does he want so much to see Jimmy? What did he say that sounded so enticing? Why doesn't he want Jimmy to get lost? Why did Blatz try to sell Jimmy something? Why did he offer to pick him up?

Does Mr. Blatz feel this when other salespeople phone? No! Why not? Because they don't act like Jimmy. They act like big shots who know everything. Jimmy acted as though it didn't matter whether Mr. Blatz made an appointment with him or not...without sounding arrogant. Mr. Blatz doesn't even know the name of Jimmy's company! What if he does get lost? He doesn't know how to track him down.

A telephone conversation can be similar to the old time radio dramas...painting images like a master painter. But, instead of using paint, brush, and canvas, Jimmy uses Theater of the Mind. Mr. Blatz' mental picture of Jimmy is exactly the picture that Jimmy wants him to have. He stands out from all the other callers. That's why they're getting together this afternoon.

Let's turn the situation around. What if you get called by someone who's as good as Jimmy? Today, there's a proliferation of professional soliciting companies utilizing the telephone to sell you a wide variety of products and services. The pitch is written so that whatever you say, there's a preprogrammed slick answer. Many products and services, such as recreational lots, magazines, vacations, time-sharing, long distance service, and memberships are sold over the phone. In sales promotion parlance, that type of telephone solicitation operation is referred to as a boiler room operation. When you get called, it's possible to turn the tables, switch the pitch, and have fun doing it. In the following situation, Jimmy Dover is on the receiving end of the phone call. Let's read what happens.

* * *

A Defense Against the Boiler Room

Jimmy Dover answered the phone. He'd been taking a nap on the couch.

"Good afternoon, Mr. Dover! This is Mr. Dover, isn't it?"

"Yes," he answered.

"Fine. I've finally reached you! I'm Miss Counter from Amalgamated Periodical Services? Am I taking you away from anything important?"

"Uh, no, well, uh, I was just taking a nap. What is it?"

"It's about your magazine subscription to Monthly Quarterly. Before we automatically renew it, we want to get your verbal permission. Nobody likes unsolicited mail."

"That right."

"We're also updating our records, Mr. Dover. May I take a minute to be absolutely certain we have your name and address right?"

"Sure."

Jimmy had a vague recollection that he'd once subscribed, but he couldn't recall seeing an issue of the magazine for several years. Jimmy was becoming more alert. He opted to make this experience enjoyable rather than an annoyance. Miss Counter was obviously up on her lines and well-trained.

"Your full name is Jimmy Dover...D-O-V-E-R. Right?"

"Right. What's your full name?"

"Miss Nellie Counter. What is your complete mailing address including zip?"

Her reply is excellent. If it's fair for you to ask questions, then it's fair for the other. Acknowledging that fact removes confrontation, and makes the caller seem more vulnerable and easy to deal with.

Jimmy had changed residences three years earlier, and he could have terminated the interview by asking her what address she had in her records. Chances are, she would have his old address. But, he didn't. He told her his current address.

"Fine," she said. "We'll be sending you an acknowledgment along with our statement."

"If I have second thoughts, can I reject it at that time?"

"We value you as a reader, Mr. Dover. Of course you may. May I take down names of any of your friends, neighbors, church members, business associates who might also consider reading Monthly Quarterly?"

"Yes, you may. Just a second. I'm going to put the phone down for a minute. I just got a flash. I'll be right back. Is that okay?"

"Of course."

Jimmy set the phone down and went into the kitchen to make a peanut butter sandwich. He decided to toast it. After an elaborate effort requiring five minutes, he returned to the phone with the sandwich in his hand. Miss Counter was waiting.

"Miss Counter?" said Jimmy.

"Yes!"

"It's taking me longer than I thought. I'll be just two more minutes."

"I'm here."

Jimmy returned to the kitchen and poured a big glass of milk. He noticed his wife's recipe box atop the refrigerator. Jimmy knew that Miss Counter's pitch depended on people's ignorance or forgetfulness, since she'd pretended that Jimmy was a current subscriber. He decided to deal with this misrepresentation without getting high blood pressure or creating a confrontation.

Miss Counter was waiting, unable to phone anyone else. If only she'd asked Jimmy how he liked the magazine. She'd left that part out of her pitch, which asked only questions that required an affirmative answer. Think about the Theater of the Mind going on in her mind about what Jimmy might be doing.

Finally, after ten minutes, Jimmy returned to the phone. "Miss Counter? I've kept you waiting too long. I thought I could put my hands right on it. I finally realized it was on top of the refrigerator. My wife likes to keep it there."

"What's that?" she asked.

"We've got this metal box, and we keep it filed alphabetically. It's quite systematic. Everything's in there. All kinds of information. Anyway, I've looked completely through the M's under Magazine Subscriptions and the P's, you know, People Who Might Be Interested in Subscribing to Magazines, and I don't find anybody in there. Not a soul! Sorry."

There was a long pause at Miss Counter's end of the line. Jimmy listened. Finally, he heard a click, then after a moment...a dial-tone.

* * *

Retail Showrooms

Approximately half of the prospects who visit retail showrooms for such products as boats, automobiles, appliances, equipment, snowmobiles, motorcycles, et al phone first. Even if only one tenth did, telephone skills are obligatory. This section is excerpted from the author's book entitled, NonConfrontation Selling...The One-on-One Revolution.

Why do prospects phone first rather than make a personal appearance? So they can be anonymous, get information, and vanish. The telephone company coined an appropriate slogan, "Let your fingers do the walking." The caller strives to get information and give none. Ironically, shortly after the caller receives the information he hangs up. Here's a typical situation.

Unskilled salesperson answers the phone.

"Sales," says the salesperson.

"Hello," says the caller. "I saw your ad for the heavy duty Maytag washer-dryer? Do you still have them?"

"Sure do," answers the salesperson. "They're right in front of me."

"Thanks," says the caller.

The line goes dead. What if the caller does show up? Does he know the salesperson's name? And vice versa?

Another typical bad situation.

"Sales department," says the salesperson.

"I'm looking at your ad for that Honda 1000 Gold Wing bike," volunteers the caller. "Is that your best price?"

"Are you kidding?" asks the salesperson. "I'm sure we can work out just about anything you want when you come in and take a look at it."

"Thanks," says the caller. "Maybe I'll drop by after work."

The line goes dead. This situation is worse than the first, because the caller has a reasonable expectation that the advertised price will be substantially reduced. If he appears, and it isn't, guess what?

Let's define two terms, Inanimate Objects and Communications.

* * *

Inanimate Objects

Three dictionary definitions:

1. Not having the qualities associated with active, living organisms.
2. Not animate.
3. Grammar. Belonging to the class of nouns that stand for nonliving things.

In both situations the salesperson was an Inanimate Object. His first greetings were "Sales" and "Sales department." When one meets an individual in person, does he say, "Sales."

Idiotic, isn't it? If so, why not by phone? Inanimate objects don't match up with prospects any more than a fencepost would, or a door, or lead weight.

* * *

Communications...a Definition

Two dictionary definitions:

1. The act of communicating, transmission.
2. a). The exchange of thoughts, messages, or information, as by speech, signals, writing, or behavior.
   b). Interpersonal rapport.
   c). The art or technique of using words effectively and with grace in imparting one's ideas.

In either situation was there any exchange of thoughts? What about interpersonal rapport? Or "grace of imparting..."? The salesperson could just as well have been the elevator voice.

The best definition:

Communications occurs from the receiver to the sender, not from the sender to the receiver. This definition is paramount. Carve it upon one's desk, graffiti on the overpass, marble letters atop the Acropolis. Once the reader accepts this premise and definition, his communication skills soar.

A wrong way.

"What's your telephone number?" asks the salesperson.

"555-2628," replies the caller.

"Thanks," asks the salesperson.

What's wrong with it? Everything! Communications occurs from the receiver to the sender, not from the sender to the receiver. In the foregoing, did the receiver of the information return it to the sender? No, he only received it.

The proper way.

"What's your telephone number?" asks the salesperson.

"555-2628," replies the caller.

"Your number is 555-2628?" clarifies the salesperson.

"That's correct," replies the caller.

The salesperson simply repeats the information he's received from the caller, and good communications occur.

Another wrong way:

"Jerry," says the boss, "I'm calling a special sales meeting for Thursday morning at 8 a.m. Be sure you notify everybody."

"Will do," says Jerry.

The following Thursday, no one shows up. The boss confronts Jerry, who explains, "I thought you meant next Thursday." The missing ingredient? The communications didn't go from the receiver to the sender.

The right way:

"Jerry," says the boss, "I'm calling a special sales meeting for Thursday morning at 8 a.m. Be sure you notify everybody."

"The meeting's this Thursday at 8 a.m.," repeats Jerry, "and, you want me to notify the sales staff and all managers?"

"That's correct," replies the boss.

"Will do," says Jerry.

The boss knows that Jerry knows, and Jerry knows that the boss knows that he knows. The meeting's less likely to go awry, and more likely to be successful. Jerry (the receiver) repeated the information back to the boss (the sender), and good communications occurred.

Another wrong way: Hotel guest phones front desk to request a wake-up call.

"Front desk," says the innkeeper.

"I'm Mr. Wayfarer in room 1416," says the caller. "Will you give me a wake-up call at 6:30?"

"Will do," replies the innkeeper. "Good night."

Will the innkeeper answer other calls before he completes this task? Will he record it accurately regardless of whether he has interruptions? Is he error-proof? Does Mr. Wayfarer know that the innkeeper knows? Will he toss and turn?

The right way:

"I certainly will, Mr. Wayfarer," replies the innkeeper. "You wish a wakeup call tomorrow morning at six thirty. Room 1416. I'm putting it in my computer as we speak. Good night, Mr. Wayfarer."

"Good night."

Good communications require very little effort or time...only discipline. Now the guest can sleep like a baby.

Recap:

1. Don't be an inanimate object.
2. Communications occur from the receiver to the sender...not from the sender to the receiver.

In the following dialogue, the salesperson practices good communications principles, puts the caller at ease, opts not to be an inanimate object, obtains and provides good information, improves the likelihood that the caller will visit the dealership and seek him out.

*   *   *

Good Phone Conversation

The salesperson picks up the phone after hearing a page that there's a call for the Sales Department.

"Hello. My name is Jimmy. Jimmy Dover. What is your name?"

"My name is Gary Shultsman."

"Shultsman. Is your last name spelled S-C-H-U-L-T-Z-M-A-N?"

"No. It's S-H-U-L-T-S-M-A-N."

"Oh. S-H-U-L-T-S-M-A-N. With an S. Sorry I misspelled it. My last name is spelled D-O-V-E-R. Dover. Jimmy Dover. Are you calling about our ad?"

"Well, yes. I see where you've got a few late-model pickups, and I wanted to see if you have any one or two year old ones with 4-wheel drive and club cab?"

"Are you calling about a vehicle like that because it's similar to the one you're presently driving?"

"No. I drive a Mustang, but I've been looking to replace it with a pickup."

"You drive a Mustang? What year is it?"

"It's a YEAR. (three years old)"

"The reason I'm sounding so exclamatory, Mr. Shultsman, is because just recently Mr. Goodfellow, our used car manager, was looking for a vehicle kind of like that for another customer. (This is a Carrot). You mean you might be thinking of selling it?"

"Well sure, if the price is right."

"Mr. Goodfellow will be very pleased to hear that. By the way, Mr. Shultsman, you cannot imagine the tremendous activity that our ad has caused at the dealership. (This is a Carrot). In fact, it's so noisy you can probably hear the commotion over the phone. Will you speak up a little bit?"

"Can you hear me better?" exclaimed Mr. Shultsman in a louder voice.

"Yes. Thank you. By the way, in case we get cut off by one of the other telephone lines, may I get your number so I can call you right back?" (This is a Carrot).

"Okay. My number is 555-8724."

"Let me write that down. 555-8274?"

"No. It's 555-8724."

"Oh. 555-8724?"

"Yes."

"Fine. By the way, Mr. Shultsman, are you calling from home?"

"Yes, I am."

"Well, let me ask you this, Mr. Shultsman, if you get a newer vehicle, will that make you a 2-vehicle family?"

"No. I'm single. One's enough."

"Well, let me ask you this, Mr. Shultsman, on your Mustang is there any equipment you particularly like that you would like to have again if you replace it with a pickup? For example, do you have a preference for a stick shift or an automatic?"

"Automatic."

"How important is air-conditioning?"

"Very important."

"What about the radio?"

"A CD would be nice this time."

"If you get a newer truck, how important would it be to be able to store things behind the driver's seat."

"Not very."

"Would anyone besides you drive it?"

"No."

"What would be an example of the heaviest load you'd have?

"My two motorcycles."

"Would you be towing anything with it?"

"I've got a 14 foot aluminum boat on a trailer."

"Do you use your Mustang now for that?"

"Yes, I have a trailer hitch."

"By the way, the dealer here, Mr. Walters, is so pleased about the tremendous response we've been getting that he's talking about repeating this same promotion next year too!" (This is a Carrot).

"That's nice."

The salesperson knows that four carrots provide excellent odds for success in obtaining an appointment. So he begins that development.

"Well, let me ask you this, Mr. Shultsman, are you looking for information about a truck because you're desirous of getting a newer vehicle right away, or are you simply making an inquiry for several months from now?"

"Oh, I'm looking to get a truck right away when I find what I'm looking for."

"You mean that if we have what you might be looking for, you'd come down today or later on this afternoon?"

"That's why I'm calling."

"Well, great! By the way, when you say today sometime, would you be thinking later on this afternoon?"

"That would be best for me?"

The salesperson knows the Match Up is complete, so it's relationship-building time.

"If you could give me an approximate time, I can see if that works good for me, too. By the way, Mr. Shultsman, would you prefer I continue referring to you by your last name?"

"Gary's fine."

"Well, thank you...Gary. Please call me Jimmy. You mean around three or four o'clock? Something like that?"

"Four will work."

"Let me check my schedule to see if that's good for me. Let me put the phone down for a moment. Is that okay?"

"Yes."

Jimmy sets the phone down and walks across the room to his planning calendar on the wall. He needs to convey to all prospects that he's always busy and has an appointment calendar, just like any professional such as a doctor or dentist or accountant. Many car-buyers believe the opposite, that salesperson sit around all day and drink coffee.

He returns to the phone. "Mr. Shultsman, I mean Gary?" he says.

"Yes?" replies Gary.

"I just checked my schedule. Four o'clock or shortly after will be perfect for me. Is that still good for you?"

"That'll work."

"Fine. Have you ever been to Walters Motors before?"

"You're on East Broadway, aren't you?"

"That's right. What direction would you be coming from at that time?"

"I'm out here at Melody Heights."

"Well, just pull into our huge driveway from Broadway and park right in front of our new vehicle showroom. When you enter the glass doors, you'll see the receptionist, Maxine, at the big white desk. Tell Maxine that you've got an appointment with me, Jimmy Dover. She'll ring my office, and I'll be right there.

Do you feel okay with those directions, Gary?"

"Yes."

"Good. I'm going to ask you one favor. You don't have to, but let me put in my request. If something should come up for you anytime between now and two o'clock that would cause you to know for certain you can't make it at four o'clock, would you please call me so I can make arrangements to see someone else at that time? And, I'll do the same for you."

"Sure. But I'll be there."

"I'm looking forward to meeting you in person."

After hanging up, the salesperson should immediately notify the Receptionist and inform her about the scheduled appointment. When the prospect arrives, the Receptionist will be expecting him.

"Hello. I've come to see Mr. Dover," says Gary to Maxine.

"Mr. Shultsman?" she says without hesitation.

"Yes."

"Mr. Dover is expecting you. Let me ring his office."

Who wouldn't like to be treated like this?

* * *

Let's reverse the situation. The receptionist is unaware of the appointment.

A wrong way:

"Hello. I've come to see Mr. Dover," says Gary to Maxine.

"Is he expecting you?" she asks.

"Yes."

"What's your name,?"

"Gary Shultsman. I talked to him just before noon."

Maxine turns to a salesperson, who is sitting near the window. "Fred, have you seen Jimmy?" she asks.

"He may have gone to lunch." replies Fred.

Is there any prospect who'd be impressed? Is Mr. Shultsman being made to feel important? Is professionalism anywhere? But, who's responsible for the receptionist knowing? Or not knowing?

*　　　　*　　　　*

Returning to the proper way, another ingredient for good appointment preparation occurs ten minutes before the appointed time. During situations when the prospect has inquired about a specific vehicle, the salesperson should arrange to park that vehicle in a highly-visible location, and attach a hand-written note to the steering wheel that reads, "Reserved for Gary Shultsman." Special people deserve special treatment. And, if a potential customer isn't special, then who is?

*　　　　*　　　　*

Moral Obligation

Asking the prospect to notify the salesperson within a reasonable period of time before the actual appointment if he can't make it…and his promise to do so…is the Moral Obligation. When the phone call includes the Moral Obligation, the odds that the prospect will appear soar; but when not included, plummet.

One reason why some appointment prospects are 'No-Shows' is they don't perceive the cost to the salesperson. The 'No-Show' believes the salesperson can simply talk to another prospect during the time period he'd booked. Reality is that the appointment causes the salesperson to preclude all other activities for about thirty minutes before to one or two hours afterward. It's problematic for the salesperson to commence another activity shortly before an appointment, because the appointment's timely appearance will interfere…and both will be compromised. Moreover, a

'No-Show' prevents a salesperson to immediately pursue other activities. Optimistic and hopeful, the salesperson waits like an expectant father for a reasonable time and cedes other opportunities. A No-Show typically costs the salesperson at least two hours of productivity. Since the 'No-Show' places no value on a salesperson's time, the onus is on the salesperson to value his own time...hence the Moral Obligation.

In the preceding dialogue, the salesperson placed value on his time by informing the caller that scheduled appointments are common practice as evidenced by his appointment book. If he'd said, "Anytime is good. I'm here until eight o'clock tonight," his time would have appeared worthless, as he's conveyed a blank slate.

"I'm going to ask you one favor." asks the salesperson. "You don't have to, but let me put in my request. If something should come up for you anytime between now and two o'clock that would cause you to know for certain you can't make it at four o'clock, would you please call me so I can make arrangements to see someone else at that time? And, I'll do the same for you."

"Sure. But I'll be there."

'Within a reasonable period of time' is subjective. When the appointment is the following morning, the dialogue can alter to:

"If something should come up for you anytime between now and this evening around dinnertime that would cause you to know for certain you can't make it..."

And if the appointment is imminent...two hours off...then:

"...If something should come up for you within the next hour that would cause you to know for certain you can't make it..."

Or if the appointment is a week from next Tuesday, then:

"...If something should come up for you anytime between now and the Friday before our appointment that would cause you to know for certain you can't make it..."

Moral Obligation must be an element of each appointment call, regardless of when, to improve the number of caller that show up as promised.

* * *

Mental Trip

The caller doesn't know what the salesperson looks like, so upon arrival anyone he sees could be Jimmy Dover. Not everyone on the sales staff makes a good first impression. Some are smokers, a few oblivious, others huddled with co-workers relating off-color stories. Is one the telephone voice? Shudder. The Mental Trip contained in the phone conversation described Maxine seated at her "big white desk" and Mr. Dover in his office. As a result, all others are invisible.

"Just pull into our huge driveway," says the salesperson, "from Broadway and park right in front of our new vehicle showroom. When you enter the glass doors, you'll see the receptionist, Maxine, at the big white desk. Tell Maxine that you've got an appointment with Jimmy Dover. She'll ring my office, and I'll be right there."

For many, visiting an retail showroom is scary, and the slightest aberration repels them. The Mental Trip prepares the caller for the best possible first impression. He visualizes driving onto the store's lot, parking in front, walking through the glass doors to Maxine's big white desk, and watching her ring Mr. Dover's office. No gauntlet of salespeople, only a yellow brick road covered with scented herbs and the highly-visible desired vehicle waiting with his name on the steering wheel.

* * *

Carrots

A Carrot, by definition, is a compelling reason for the caller to visit the retail showroom. Here's a Carrot list.

1. Special Event
2. Special Purchase
3. Factory Rebate
4. Lower Interest Rates
5. Special Selection
6. Year-End Clearance
7. Crowded showroom
8. Too much inventory
9. Desired product is available
10. Response exceeds expectations
11. Busy phone lines may get cut off
12. Several others to choose from
13. Special financing available
14. Size of company
15. Repeating promotion by acclamation
16. And on and on.

General Rule: Always give the caller four carrots before requesting an appointment. If the salesperson offers only one carrot, the caller probably won't come in. Even if he does, he usually won't remember the salesperson's name. This is one of the more difficult telephone disciplines to maintain, because the salesperson gets excited as soon as the caller sounds cooperative.

* * *

Getting Derailed

"Hello, my name is Barry Rogers," says the salesperson as he picks up the phone. "What is your name?"

"My name is Rose Matthews," replies the caller.

"Thanks for calling, Rose Mathews. Is your last name spelled M-A-T-H-E-W-S?"

"No. It has two T's."

"Oh. M-A-T-T-H-E-W-S. Sorry I misspelled it. My last name is spelled R-O-G-E-R-S. Rogers. Are you calling about our ad?"

"No. Late last night I drove by and noticed the French Provincial living room grouping in your front window? If you still have it, I want to stop by after work in a couple of hours to look at it."

"We still have it, Ms Matthews. Be sure to ask for Barry."

"Okay. Goodbye."

What's wrong? The caller offered her name without opposition. She volunteered to appear. Good start, but consider that she may be calling other dealerships. The only information the salesperson obtained was her name and that she's employed. When Rose got the information she sought, she hung up. Retread the dialogue and confirm it contains just one Carrot...Desired vehicle is available. Three Carrots to go, and in Rose's case, they would have been easily obtained.

*   *   *

Back On Track (following the introduction)

"Are you calling about our ad?" asks Jimmy Dover.

"No," replies Rose. "Late last night I drove by and noticed that two year old Dodge minivan...the green one? If you still have it, I want to stop by after work in a couple of hours to look at it."

"Is one of the reasons you're interested in looking at the minivan," asks Jimmy, "because it's similar to the vehicle you're presently driving?"

"No. I drive a Buick Century, but it's not big enough now for our three kids."

"Do any of them drive?"

"Omigosh, no. My oldest is only seven years old."

"How old is your Buick Century?"

"It's a MAKE/MODEL." (four years old)

"The reason I'm sounding so exclamatory, Ms Matthews, is because just recently Mr. Goodfellow, our used car manager, was looking for a vehicle kind of like that for another customer. (This is a Carrot). You mean you might be thinking of selling it?"

"That's our plan."

"Mr. Goodfellow will be very pleased to hear that. By the way, Ms Matthews, you cannot imagine the tremendous activity that our ad has caused at the dealership. (This is a Carrot). In fact, it's so noisy you can probably hear the commotion over the phone. Will you speak up a little bit?"

"Can you hear me better?" she exclaimed in a louder voice."

"Yes. Thank you. By the way, in case we get cut off by one of the other telephone lines, may I get your number so I can call you right back?" (This is a Carrot).

"My number is 555-8724."

"Let me write that down. 555-8274?"

"No. It's 555-8724."

"Oh. 555-8724?"

"Yes."

"Fine. By the way, Ms Matthews, are you calling from work?"

"Yes, but please call me Rose."

"Well, let me ask you this, Rose, if you get a newer vehicle, will that make you a 2-vehicle family?"

"Yes. My husband drives his Ford pickup."

"A Ford pickup? Wow. What year is it?"

"It's a MAKE/MODEL." (two years old)

"Well, let me ask you this, Rose, on your Buick is there any equipment you particularly like that you'd like to have again if you replace it with a minivan? For example, do you have a preference for a stick shift or an automatic?"

"Automatic."

"How important is air-conditioning?"

"Very important."

"What about the radio?"

"A CD would be nice."

Rose has not yet learned whether the green minivan is still available, but the salesperson has obtained much information about her and her wants, as he's asked her three FBI Interrogation School Questions already.

"I feel so lucky, Rose," replies the Jimmy, " because based on what you've told me, there's more than one minivan that fits your description that you can take a look at. (This is a Carrot). How soon after you get off work can you be here?"

The salesperson has been counting the carrots, and he's up to four. The time is ripe to ask for an appointment.

"I'm only fifteen minutes away," replies Rose. "I get off work at five thirty."

"Are you saying sometime between five forty-five and six-o'clock?"

"Yes."

"Let me check my schedule to see if that's good for me. Let me put the phone down for a moment. Is that okay?"

"Yes."

Jimmy sets the phone down and walks across the room to his planning calendar on the wall, then returns to the phone.

"Rose?" he says.

"Yes?"

"I just checked my schedule. Just before six o'clock or shortly thereafter is a good time. Is that still good for you?"

"Perfect."

"What direction will you be coming from?"

"My office is downtown in the Hastings Building.

"Well, just pull into our huge driveway from Broadway and park right in front of our new vehicle showroom. When you enter the glass doors, you'll see the receptionist, Maxine, at the big white desk. Tell Maxine that you've got an appointment with me, Jimmy Dover. She'll ring my office, and I'll be right there.

Do you feel okay with those directions, Rose?"

"Yes."

"Good," says Jimmy. "I'm going to ask you one favor. You don't have to, but let me put in my request. If something should come up for you anytime between now and four o'clock that would cause you to know for certain you can't make it at around six, would you please call me so I can make arrangements to see someone else at that time? And, I'll do the same for you."

"Sure. But I'll be there."

"I'm looking forward to meeting you in person. Carve my name in your desk."

"I already have. It's Jimmy Dover."

By not omitting any principles or taking shortcuts (even when an appointment seemed assured) the salesperson reduced the chances this caller would phone any competitors before the appointed time, obtained more information about the caller and a better description of the desired product, held out for at least four carrots before requesting an appointment, and included the Mental Trip and the Moral Obligation.

The telephone is a fabulous instrument, giving anyone the power to suggest a wide range of characteristics. When the telephone evolves into a television phone, it will eliminate opportunities for developing Theater of the Mind in the same way old time dramatic radio passed into relative obscurity with the advent of television.

Chapter Six

Non-Negotiable Factors

The Villains

Many people believe that goods and services cost dearly because sellers are making outlandish profits. It's difficult for a prospect to make a favorable buying decision when that's his perception.

Do you recall ever happily paying too much for a product or service? It doesn't matter whether you actually did pay too much, only that you believe you did. A product may seem irresistible, but if you don't buy it because of high price, then it's resistible. A Rolls Royce, for example, might seem irresistible, but if you don't buy one because of its huge price, it's resistible.

If you were interested in a winter coat that cost five hundred dollars, and the seller offered it to you for his wholesale cost, you might conclude that it was a good deal...and you could then concentrate on whether or not you liked the coat, instead of fretting about the seller's markup.

Selling prices are influenced by factors such as manufacturing costs, taxes, shipping, finance charges, government regulations and selling costs. Most are non-negotiable. The more Non-Negotiable Factors that are included in the selling price, the less chance that the prospect will believe he's being overcharged. Therefore, creating an awareness of Non-Negotiable Factors increases a product's appeal.

If you recently purchased a major item such as a kitchen appliance, boat, automobile, remodeling, heavy equipment, or a new residence, think about how much less it would have cost if you'd purchased it three years ago. In the interim, taxes, inflation, finance charges, and government regulations have ganged up to cause sizable price increases. Because all of them are Non-Negotiable Factors, none can be eliminated from the selling price. Let's examine why.

* * *

1. Sales Tax. Can one prospect pay less sales tax than another? If the sales tax is 5% in your state, for example, can another person pay 4% or 3% or 2%? Of course not! All must pay the same sales tax rate. It applies equally to all.
2. Inflation. If inflation is 4% per year, can some products be subject to only 3% or 2%? Of course not! All are subject to the same inflation rate.
3. Finance Charges. If the annualized percentage rate at the bank is 9% under normal competitive conditions, can the average borrower be charged 3% or 7%? Of course not! There's very little that even the most creditworthy borrower can do to substantially alter the current rate. Finance charges are basically non-negotiable.
4. Government Regulations. If a new law has caused the cost of a product or service to increase, can some prospects subtract the cost of the government-mandated add-ons from the price? Of course not! All are subject to the same government regulations. They're non-negotiable. The price of an automobile is very government regulation-filled, because it includes the cost of such items as emission-control devices, safety bumpers, seat belts, air bags, steel-reinforced doors and frames, gas tank protection, safety glass and dozens of other government-regulated items. Eliminating them would reduce the price by thousands of dollars. But, no seller can eliminate them. They've become part of the product's selling price, and they're non-negotiable.

Just imagine. A businessman gets an idea for a new store that will only sell government regulations . He believes that their proliferation in recent years has caused the public to yearn for them. If not so, he reasons, why so many? At his Grand Opening he waits and waits. No one shows up. No one wants any. And no one will deny that they cause inflation.

There are certainly other non-negotiable factors. How about the Cost of Materials?

* * *

Cost of Materials

What a project! Keenan and Mary Fawcett planned to remodel their kitchen and downstairs bathroom, and they realized they'd need a plumber, so they phoned Percy's Plumbing for a bid on the job. Percy knew all about Non-Negotiable Factors.

He listened patiently and took notes while Keenan and Mary showed him the scope of the project.

"What will it cost?" asked Keenan.

"I love working with residential customers," replied Percy. "When I don't work, I don't get paid. You know how it is. I'm very receptive to the prospect of having a job that will keep me busy in one place for three or four days straight."

Keenan looked at Mary and smiled.

"I've added this all up," continued Percy, "and the entire cost will amount to $6,751.60. The materials amount to seventy percent of the total, and labor is the other thirty percent. I can't do much about the cost of materials, but I can work with you on the labor cost. Ten percent of my labor would make it a little tight for me, but that would be all right, I guess." Perry sighed.

He's reduced the negotiable amount from one hundred percent to thirty percent of the whole cost by positioning the cost of materials as Non-Negotiable Factors! Hence, a ten percent discount is ten percent of thirty percent...or three percent altogether!

* * *

Perfect Pitch

Jimmy Dover looked at his watch. He owned the automobile dealership and knew about sticker shock...the sinking feeling prospects get when they discover the vehicle's cost. One of Jimmy's salespeople, Jerry, was at that moment trying to sell a new car to Mr. and Mrs. Johnson, who were suffering from sticker shock and believed that the selling price contained too much profit. They weren't certain how much, but they'd read somewhere it was a lot.

Jimmy had been conducting sales training sessions the past two weeks to his staff, and two topics were sticker shock and Non-Negotiable Factors. He'd informed the staff that any prospect suffering from sticker shock should be introduced to him, so that he could demonstrate the effective remedy. Jerry followed the instructions and brought his prospects into Jimmy's office.

"I want to compliment you for considering your purchase now instead of waiting," said Jimmy. "Your present vehicle will never be worth more than it is today. All used vehicles decline in value every day; and every new vehicle, regardless of the make, continue to get more expensive. The factories are always raising the prices to us dealers. Some days I'm afraid to look at my E-mail. It's really getting awful. You've complimented me personally by considering my dealership for your new car. Thank you. May I take a few moments right now to show you firsthand what car buyers are facing today?"

They nodded.

"Thank you," said Jimmy. "There's a serious problem going on in this country...so serious, in fact, that it causes most of us to, well, lay awake nights. And, that problem is inflation."

Jimmy's countenance was like that of a hound dog, expressing sadness, bewilderment, and concern. Jimmy placed his closed hand to his chest, and looked down, crushing his tie, as if to cough.

"I'm sorry," he said. "Excuse me. Don't ever have Dr. Pepper for breakfast. I'll be okay. Would you care for some?"

"No, thank you," replied Mrs. Johnson. She smiled.

"Well anyway," said Jimmy, "I don't know how inflation has affected you, but it seems like every few months, people who are on fixed incomes get a great big bite taken out of their take-home pay. Last quarter, for example, it was more than two percent. The quarter before that...the same. That means if it keeps up, by year's end it will total possibly seven or eight percent. And even though it probably hasn't averaged that much every year, it's not hard to believe that even averaging five or six percent per year that the cost of everything has gone up fifteen to twenty percent over the past three or four years...just from inflation! And, you can't imagine the number of people...they think they want to get a new car...they come to the dealership...not just here, but all over the country...they find one they like...then discover what it costs...and go into a state of shock. They say to themselves, 'Maybe I'll take two or three thousand dollars out of my savings account and go ahead and get my old car fixed up.' You can hardly blame them! That's terrible for business. That's why we lay awake nights."

* * *

Inflation is a Non-Negotiable Factor. Jimmy is informing the prospects how much of the total selling price is caused by inflation...fifteen to twenty percent. Keep in mind that Jimmy's objective is to sell the vehicle for retail price, not some enormously-discounted figure. He knows he must have as many Non-Negotiable Factors as possible to justify the selling price.

Let's say that three years ago the prospects bought and financed a new vehicle for monthly payments of three hundred dollars. Let's say also that inflation averaged five percent per year. That means the cost of goods and services went up by fifteen percent just from inflation. Financing the higher figure would cause the monthly payment to increase by the same percentage to three hundred forty five dollars. Profit had nothing to do with the forty five dollar per month increase. Inflation was the culprit.

Prospects' attitudes change when they're informed about Non-Negotiable Factors. Many realize there is not so much to bargain for as they thought, and their expectations for huge discounts are diminished.

Jimmy could have taken some verbal shortcuts to explain inflation, but it wouldn't have been so effective. He could have simply said, "Vehicles have gone up in price about fifteen percent since you bought your last one three years ago just from inflation, and that's why the one you're looking at seems so expensive."

Instead, though, Jimmy built a brick house.

*　　　　*　　　　*

Stacking the Bricks

Let's back up in the conversation, define a Brick House, and read how Jimmy builds it...one brick at a time.

Jimmy:

"I don't know how inflation has affected you, but it seems like every few months, people who are on fixed incomes get a great big bite taken out of their take-home pay. Last quarter, for example, it was more than two percent.

This is the first brick...two percent! Jimmy will lay the next brick.

Jimmy:

"The quarter before that...the same."

That's the second brick. Then annualized for a whole year.

Jimmy:

"That means if it keeps up, by year's end it will total possibly seven or eight percent."

Jimmy is building the brick house by Stacking the Bricks very carefully. No hyperbole. Everyone believes inflation is too high. Everyone knows what it is. Everyone believes it's even higher than Jimmy indicates. Jimmy is getting agreement from the Johnson. His basic premises build the foundation for his case, in the same way a good prosecuting attorney lays out evidence.

Jimmy:

"And even though it probably hasn't averaged that much every year, it's not hard to believe that even averaging five or six percent per year that the cost of everything has gone up fifteen to twenty percent over the past three or four years...just from inflation!

He finally presents the entire brick house in one sentence. Once the prospects know that the cost of a product or service is caused by things other than profit, they'll be more realistic about their expectations for a good deal; and they'll begin considering whether or not they like the product instead of how much they don't like the price.

Often, salespeople do not point out inflation as the primary cause of high prices. The unrealistic prospects can then intimidate the salesperson with, "Keep my payments below three hundred dollars, and we'll do business!"

Even Houdini couldn't do that.

* * *

Another Non-Negotiable Factor is bank interest. Dependent upon the state of the economy, bank interest rates can take violent swings. Just since 1980, they've varied from a high of twenty two percent to less than one percent, for an average of somewhere between seven and twelve percent. In the following situation, an impatient businessman, who tries to intimidate a friendly banker, discovers that a Non-Negotiable Factor stands in his way.

* * *

Unstuffy Banker

The bank lobby was elegant. Each loan officer had a highly-polished, carved-legged walnut desk with matching, squeaking chair. Six desks with six loan officers occupied the left rear area of the lobby next to the massive vault. Usually, all six desks were occupied, and since they were only eight feet apart, loan applicants had to resort to throaty whispers and heavy breathing to maintain any privacy for their financial affairs.

Sitting at one of them, Jimmy Dover watched his secretary approach. She also worked for the five other loan officers as well as their boss, Hy Price, the vice-president.

"Mr. Mike Mallis is here, Mr. Dover," she said. "He asked for Mr. Price, but when I told him he wasn't here right now, he said he'd be willing to see you."

"Send him in," replied Jimmy.

Mike Mallis owned a furniture store. His bad manners caused him to be not well-liked at the bank. Jimmy knew him by reputation, but had never dealt with him before.

Jimmy stood up as he approached. "Mr. Mallis? I'm Jimmy Dover. How are you today?" He held out his hand.

"Not very good. Man, you guys sure know how to charge for your money. It's killing me at the store! I'm thinking about changing banks."

Mallis sat down next to Jimmy's desk without shaking hands. Jimmy sat down, too. As he did so, he leaned back too far and had to struggle to keep from falling backwards. Mike Mallis reached out for him without thinking.

"Whew! Almost did it that time," said Jimmy. "This darned chair. I can't ever get it adjusted right. Just a second."

Jimmy knelt beside his chair and reached underneath it for the adjusting lever. "It's so darned tight, I don't think I can get it any tighter."

"Let me see it," replied Mr. Mallis. He knelt down beside Jimmy, who continued to try to turn the lever.

"It's stuck," said Jimmy.

"I think you're turning it the wrong way. Let me try it."

Mr. Mallis grabbed the lever and twisted it the opposite direction. It began to turn.

"There. I've got it. We'll just keep turning it until it gets tight again. There. It's getting tighter. Try it now!"

Jimmy arose from the floor, sat down and leaned back gingerly. Mr. Mallis lay stretched out on the floor on his back under the chair.

"It's much better," said Jimmy. "A little bit more."

"I can feel the pressure." Mike continued to turn the lever.

"That's even better."

"One more quarter turn. Remember to turn it clockwise."

"Wrong way doesn't work."

Mike got up from the floor and sat down.

"I sure wish you'd talk the bank into getting new furniture," said Jimmy.

"We'd make you a pretty good deal," replied Mike.

"Beside the problem of money costs you're facing right now, are your profit margins holding up pretty well?"

"They're down a little, but we've been managing. I run a pretty tight ship, you know."

"In today's economy, only the best survive."

"We plan to be around for a long time."

Jimmy leaned forward in a confidential manner. "I'm not too familiar with the retail furniture business, Mr. Mallis. What kind of gross profit margins do you work on?"

Mr. Mallis coughed. "During normal times we try to maintain forty to fifty percent gross profit."

"Some of your products have higher margins, though, don't they?"

"Of course."

"When you offer what you consider to be a good deal, Mr. Mallis, do you consider reducing your gross profit margin to about half that or even less? I hope my question doesn't sound too naive."

Mr. Mallis coughed again. "Depending on the circumstances."

"I wish we could do that."

"Do what?"

"Maintain that kind of gross profit margin. And have the luxury of altering it depending on the circumstances. Everyone believes that when interest rates are up, the bank makes a killing. I wish that were true. During normal times, to use your phrase, we try for a spread of five or six percent. If we made forty to fifty percent margin, we sure wouldn't be sitting around with this old furniture, that's for sure? And a five or six percent spread is mighty skinny, even during normal times. We certain can't make it up somewhere else when we keep offer free checking."

Mike Mallis stared at Jimmy. He was speechless.

"And when the so-called prime rate goes up, we don't even do that well. Two or three points maybe! To the most creditworthy. Minus losses for bad loans. The furniture business sounds…well…fabulous in comparison."

Mike Mallis continued to stare. Jimmy opened his bottom left desk drawer and pulled out a small yellow box. He opened and held it out to him.

"Milk Dud?"

"No thanks."

Jimmy popped one into his mouth.

"Sure?"

"No, but thanks anyway."

Jimmy closed the box and returned it to his desk drawer.

"Are you here on furniture store business today, Mr. Mallis?"

"No. I'm getting a new boat, and I want to arrange financing. It's pretty expensive."

"No problem, unless, of course, a nine percent rate is going to stop you."

Mike Mallis looked away from Jimmy and bit his lip. "No...that's not going to stop me."

"What kind of boat is it?"

* * *

Mike Mallis couldn't intimidate Jimmy with his empty threat of changing banks. Jimmy ignored it. Threats are often bluster. Instead, Jimmy enlisted him to help fix the chair. After all, he was a furniture man, who for a brief moment lay under Jimmy's chair like a bearskin rug. Jimmy's engaging conversation encouraged Mallis to brag about his furniture store's gross profit margins (even his good deals), which Jimmy contrasted to the bank's. After that, how could Mallis complain about the bank's high interest rates? Jimmy's handling of the situation caused the bank's interest rate to be recognized as a Non-Negotiable Factor.

* * *

Has this ever happened to you? A friend arrives at your house to take you out to dinner. He asks, "Where would you like to eat? You name it. By the way, I had steak for lunch today with the boss. Last night I ate pasta. There's a great seafood place about two miles from here. There's another great seafood restaurant about thirty minutes away. But, I've been working so hard this week, I think a long drive would do me in. And I'm really hungry. What do you think? Where would you like to go?"

What can you say? His invitation is permeated with Non-Negotiable Factors. You can't have steak. You can't have pasta. You can't choose a restaurant more than two miles away. You know he wants seafood. He's taken all the negotiable factors out of the discussion and boiled everything down to his choice…not yours. Who has control over where and what to eat?

Learning to recognize and use Non-Negotiable Factors effectively can help you have more control in many areas of your life.

Chapter Seven

Cliffhangers

The Edge

Cliffhangers cause a prospect to be unable to resist an idea, because if he does, he'll fall off the cliff, and the idea or transaction being discussed will be terminated. For the prospect not to fall off the cliff, he must try to give you the answer he believes you want to hear; but since its not one he's ready to give, he replies with an in-between, gray answer.

Once you know that the person you're dealing with likes what you're offering but is resisting part of the proposal...such as the price or some other detail...it's time to consider the use of a Cliffhanger.

Think about a person standing on the edge of a sheer cliff. His misstep will cause him to fall. It's scary. A Cliffhanger verbally positions him on the cliff's edge and describes the circumstances that will cause him to fall off. When asked the Cliffhanger question, the prospect will usually choose to step to safety. Typical answers practically never contain a "yes" or "no," but instead "maybe" or "possibly." No one purposely steps off a cliff. That's why they're successful.

* * *

New House

The house was magnificent. Everything seemed picture perfect. Harold and Helen Homesteader loved it from the first moment they saw it with the real estate broker, Jimmy Dover. The colonial-style house on one acre had a manicured yard and circular driveway. The Homesteaders weren't certain they'd be able to obtain normal mortgage financing, due to some past credit difficulties, so they were looking for owner financing.

"Nice," said Helen, as Jimmy stopped the car out front.

"Yes, it is," replied Jimmy. "The present owner, Mr. Castle, is one of the most meticulous perfectionists I've ever met. He considers his home his palace, and he has spared no expense to make it comfortable and unique. He's also the most difficult person I've gotten a listing from. No deviation. No compromise. Know what I mean?"

The Homesteaders looked at each other. Jimmy exited the car.

When they toured the property and discovered that the house lived up to its reputation, the Homesteaders opted to make an offer on it.

* * *

Real estate agents live with a constant, professional dilemma. Since they represent both the buyer and the seller when they're selling a property that they've also listed, they must convince the seller at listing time that they can sell it quickly for the best possible price. On the other hand, they must convince their buyer clients that they can help them purchase the property at a fair market price. In recent years, agency regulations have been enacted that requires all parties in the transaction to be made aware of and consent to what is referred to as double-agency…representing both the buyer and the seller on a single transaction; but arguably, the suspicion lingers that since the agent's commission is more when the selling price is more, if there is a bias by the agent in the transaction, it's toward the seller's interests rather than the buyer's.

When Jimmy listed Castle's house for $175,000, he reminded Mr. Castle that some sellers purposely list their houses for more than they actually believe they can sell it for so that they can "appear" to be willing to negotiate when they counteroffer.

He informed them, though, that when the asking prices are above market value, there's a dearth of lookers; and that it's best to price at actual market value, because homes in the area that are properly priced sell for about 98% of asking price. Mr. Castle, initially, was an example of many unrealistic sellers who allow greed and avarice to overtake their judgment, price it too high, and cause the property to sit ignored and unsold. Unfortunately, for many of those improperly priced properties, when their selling prices finally are reduced to market value, they're considered stale, not fresh, and don't excite the army of realtors in the area that are, instead, showing other properties that have been properly priced in the first place.

Jimmy's suggestions prevailed that since Mr. Castle's house was so perfect and well-kept that he put it on the market at the price he expected to get for it. This put more pressure on Jimmy to sell it for the asking price. Mr. Castle liked Jimmy for his gutsy recommendation. It was the primary cause for Castle to hire him as his real estate agent.

The author has met real estate people whose approaches are questionable. Their opening pitch to a potential buyer regarding a specific listed property goes something like this. "Even though the seller listed the house for $195,000, he'll take less. He's anxious to sell, and if your offer is, say, $175,000, I believe he'll strongly consider it."

This is a serious breech of the seller/agency relationship...and may only be done with the seller's prior approval. Another problem with this approach is that the asking price has dropped before the buyer even asks. The most inexperienced buyer will realize that when a price drops before he asks, it will drop even more after he asks. Does the value of anything go up or down when the price plummets like a rock for no apparent reason. Isn't a prospect likely to wonder, "What's wrong with it?"

Suppose a real estate agent is trying to sell your house. Would you prefer for him to sell the value of your house or how fast the price will plummet? It's a good rule that the agent who represents both the buyer and seller not say anything to either party that he doesn't want the other to hear.

* * *

Jimmy explained to the Homesteaders that Mr. Castle was willing to carry a contract if he was cashed out for his equity. This meant Harold and Helen could either come up with $80,000 cash or refinance. They all knew that owner financing was their goal. Harold revealed they had $35,000 from the sale of their last house.

After touring the property, they returned to Jimmy's car.

"Even though Mr. Castle is the type of seller who is inflexible," said Jimmy, "there are generally two areas of any transaction that represent the most appeal to any seller...price or terms. One will turn him on. Most sellers...I can't say whether this would be true of Mr. Castle...like one better than the other when both can't be obtained. Which would he rather have...his asking price with little down and carry the balance on a contract, or $80,000 cash in his pocket from the proceeds of regular mortgage financing...less his closing costs, of course? You'd be amazed, Harold and Helen, how many house sales ride on just those two things, regardless of how inflexible the seller might be! Here, let me roll down the window a little bit. Are you comfortable, Helen and Harold?"

They nodded.

"Can you see yourself in this house?" asked Jimmy.

"It's very exciting," said Helen. She glanced at Harold.

"I recommend that your offer reflect what the seller needs and requires...$175,000. You may think it odd for me to say it, but this particular home is underpriced based on the current market and comparables in the area. If you don't agree, then making an offer to this seller will be a big waste of time."

"We like the house, Jimmy," said Harold, but our available cash falls far short of $80,000...and we have an additional problem."

Jimmy waited.

"New furniture will cost us at least $10,000," said Harold. "That's coming out of our available cash. We've got our old stuff, of course, but Helen wants all new."

"Mmm," said Jimmy. "That makes it more difficult. But, even though the seller is tough, he doesn't have another offer in front of him. If you offered his asking price, that would achieve one of his two requirements. Nothing will occur if you don't try. I'd be willing to present it to him if you want me to?"

As they sat together in Jimmy's vehicle, they wrote an offer to buy the house.

It read in part:

$25,000 Cash Down Payment

150,000 Real Estate Contract with Mr. Castle

$175,000 PURCHASE PRICE

* * *

Two hours later, Jimmy found Mr. Castle in the locker room at the Downtown Racquetball Club preparing for a match.

"Sell my house yet, Jimmy?"

"I've got good news, and I've got bad news. What first?"

"The good news."

"I've got a family who has made an offer."

"How much?"

"$175,000."

"What's the bad news?"

"Getting all your equity out with a contract. Home buyers seeking owner contracts just aren't walking around with that much cash. These certainly aren't."

"That's what I need."

"That's why I didn't come in here waving their offer like an idiot. I've been candid with them. These nice folks don't have that much cash. Hope I didn't delay your match. I'd better get going. They're going to be disappointed. Shall I tell them to put your house out of their mind?"

"What amount of cash do they have?"

"A lot for them, not enough for you. More important than that is another question, and quite frankly, if you can't answer it appropriately, there's really no reason to present the offer to you. I can't think of any other way to ask it other than to simply blurt it out. May I?"

"I'm listening."

"Here goes. How difficult would it be for you…yes, this is a good way to ask the question, how difficult would it be for you to consider a full price offer with lesser cash than you've indicated down on an owner contract?"

"That would be difficult."

"Well, let me ask you this then. Just how difficult would it be?"

"How much cash did they offer?"

"Not very much."

"How much is that?"

"Twenty-five thousand."

"Let me see the offer."

Jimmy showed him the paperwork.

"I might go for half of the eighty thousand," said Castle after two minutes.

"That'll kill it. What do you mean by half of eighty thousand?"

"Forty thousand."

"Yes. That'll kill it."

"I need cash myself from this transaction, Jimmy. I'll accept thirty five thousand, but anything less just won't work for me."

"I'll present your counteroffer if you'd like me to."

Jimmy and Castle walked together toward the racquetball court. Jimmy made the changes in the offer, and Castle signed the document as he held it up against the wall of the locker room.

"I'll get back to you," said Jimmy

"Good luck."

Jimmy used the lobby phone to call Harry at work.

"Did he like our offer?" asked Harry.

"We're making progress. Let's get together tonight or sometime tomorrow at your place."

"Tonight will work."

"Eight o'clock?"

"We'll be there."

* * *

At eight o'clock, Jimmy knocked on their door. Helen let him in and seated him at the dining room table across from Harold, who was looking at a furniture catalog.

"I've prepared a little treat," said Helen as she set brownies and coffee on the table. "Harold tells me that you met with the seller today."

"He was receptive to the owners contract aspect of your offer. We've made progress, but I've got something very important to ask that I'm afraid affects the house deal."

Helen and Harold glanced at each other. She sat down.

"It's hard for me to convey," said Jimmy. "Before I do, I'd like to ask you a question. It's so important that, quite frankly, if we can't come up with the right answer, well, we might just as well forget all about this particular house deal."

"What's the question?" asked Harold.

Jimmy sighed and took a deep breath. "Well, I can't think of any other way to ask it, so, I'll just blurt it out. How difficult would it be for you…yes, this is a good way to ask the question. How difficult would it be for you to temporarily forego your new furniture?"

"That would be difficult," replied Harold.

"Well, let me ask you this then," said Jimmy. Just how difficult would it be?"

Helen smiled. "Is that all that's wrong?"

Harold gazed at her in surprise. "You've been counting on getting new furniture, honey. I promised."

She ignored him. "Jimmy, are you saying that the seller is willing to carry a contract but wants more than twenty-five thousand down?"

"Yes."

"I'd much rather have the house than the new furniture," she said. "We can always get new furniture later."

"I thought," said Harold, "that your heart was set on new furniture."

She laughed and touched his cheek. "I thought your heart was set on getting it for me."

Jimmy could recall a short story by O' Henry with a similar plot.

"How exactly did the seller want to change the offer?" asked Helen.

Jimmy showed them the counteroffer asking for $35,000 down.

"Looks good to me," said Helen.

"Me, too," said Harold.

"What a relief," said Jimmy. "I was so worried about your new furniture."

Everybody laughed.

"May I fill up your cup?" asked Helen.

* * *

Let's read how Jimmy set up Cliffhangers for the buyers and the seller.

Jimmy:

"I've got good news, and I've got bad news. What first?"

Castle:

"The good news."

Jimmy:

"I've got a family who has made an offer."

Castle:

"How much?"

Jimmy:

"$175,000."

Castle:

"What's the bad news?"

Jimmy:

"Getting all your equity out with a contract. Home buyers seeking owner contracts just aren't walking around with that much cash. These certainly aren't."

Castle:

"That's what I need."

Both are exhibiting the Guts to Fail. Jimmy's next statement will position Castle on the edge of the cliff. To keep from falling off, Castle will need to give Jimmy the answer he wants to hear...even though it won't be a "yes" or "no." If he says "no," Jimmy will leave immediately and abort the deal.

Jimmy:

"That's why I didn't come in here waving their offer like an idiot. I've been candid with them. These nice folks don't have that much cash. Hope I didn't delay your match. I'd better get going. They're going to be disappointed. Shall I tell them to put your house out of their mind?"

Castle:

"What amount of cash do they have?"

He's not so adamant as he was only seconds earlier. Jimmy discerns this and is ready with his Cliffhanger.

Jimmy:

"A lot for them, not enough for you. More important than that is another question, and quite frankly, if you can't answer it appropriately, there's really no reason to present the offer to you. I can't think of any other way to ask it other than to simply blurt it out. May I?"

He's informing Castle that if he doesn't give the right answer, it's all over. He'll fall off the cliff anyway. For Castle not to, he must give Jimmy the answer he believes Jimmy wants to hear.

Castle:

"I'm listening."

Jimmy:

"Here goes. How difficult would it be for you...yes, this is a good way to ask the question, how difficult would it be for you to consider a full price offer with lesser cash than you've indicated down on an owner contract?"

Castle:

"That would be difficult."

Castle doesn't like the edge. He steps to safety by repeating the word difficult instead of rejecting the offer outright.

Jimmy:

"Well, let me ask you this then. Just how difficult would it be?"

Castle:

"How much cash did they offer?"

They trade 'degree questions' with each other and avoid specific amounts or outright rejection.

Jimmy:

"Not very much."

Castle:

"How much is that?"

He keeps walking along the precipice very carefully to keep the matter alive.

Jimmy:

"Twenty-five thousand."

Castle:

"Let me see the offer."

He bides his time as he peers over the edge at the bottom.

Castle:

"I might go for half of the eighty thousand."

Jimmy:

"That'll kill it. What do you mean by half of eighty thousand?"

This is classic Guts to Fail language. This takes courage by Jimmy. If Castle wants to step off the edge, he can do so by making forty thousand dollars non-negotiable.

Castle:

"Forty thousand."

Jimmy:

"Yes. That'll kill it."

Jimmy isn't afraid to keep the cliff's edge right in front of Castle.

Castle:

"I need cash myself from this transaction, Jimmy. I'll accept thirty five thousand, but anything less just won't work for me."

Castle blinked. Selling his house right away is more important to him than holding out for eighty thousand dollars cash in hand. The agent knows how much cash the buyer has, but the seller doesn't. The agent knows, too, that the seller has not exceeded it, and a viable deal is not only possible now, but probable.

Jimmy:

"I'll present your counteroffer if you'd like me to."

* * *

That evening, when Jimmy visits the buyers, he utilizes a Cliffhanger that's practically verbatim the dialogue he had with Castle. Buying signs are anticipation, the furniture catalog, and the treat.

Helen:

"I've prepared a little treat. Harold tells me that you met with the seller today."

Jimmy:

"He was receptive to the owners contract aspect of your offer. We've made progress, but I've got something very important to ask that I'm afraid affects the house deal."

The Cliffhanger has begun. He'll now describe it and cause Harold and Helen to stand at its edge. It's scary.

Jimmy:

"It's hard for me to convey. Before I do, I'd like to ask you a question. It's so important that, quite frankly, if we can't come up with the right answer, well, we might just as well forget all about this particular house deal."

Just like in a soap opera, we can wonder whether the Homesteaders will want the house more than they'll want to say "no" to something.

Harold:

"What's the question?"

Jimmy:

"Well, I can't think of any other way to ask it, so, I'll just blurt it out. How difficult would it be for you...yes, this is a good way to ask the question. How difficult would it be for you to temporarily forego your new furniture?"

Jimmy is telling them that if they don't give the right answer, it's all over...they'll fall off the cliff. The key word for their saving answer is "difficult." He hasn't asked whether they can or cannot forego the furniture, but instead how difficult it would be.

The key word in a Cliffhanger question is imperative. It's the one that allows the prospect to reply with a safe answer. When the question is, "How difficult would it be?" the reply becomes, "That would be difficult," instead of "I won't do it." To succeed with a Cliffhanger, you must allow for maybe answers instead of no answers by inserting the key word into the question. The word difficult is a good one to use. It's not possible at this point in the conversation for Harold and Helen to reply that they'll not forego their furniture, or else the transaction will be over. They will have stepped off the cliff. They must give an in-between saving answer to keep the transaction alive.

Harold:

"That would be difficult."

Now, Jimmy must soften up the word difficult.

Jimmy:

"Well, let me ask you this then. Just how difficult would it be?"

Helen:

"Is that all that's wrong?"

Helen doesn't like the edge. She steps to absolute safety before Harold answers. When prospects discover that the Cliffhanger question is not such a big thing to worry about, they feel relieved...even joyful. Helen's comment, even though directed at Jimmy, communicates an important message to Harold...that she wants the new house more than she wants the new furniture. Harold puts up a weak facade.

Harold:

"You've been counting on getting new furniture, honey. I promised."

The use of pronouns is helpful there to determine intention. If he'd been counting on getting new furniture, he would have used "we" or "I." Think about how much stronger this statement could have been if either one of them had said, "I've been counting on getting new furniture. You promised." Very assertive. Instead, Harold is now relieved, because he realizes the furniture isn't so important to Helen, and he's off the hook. Jimmy is relieved, too. He's almost got a commitment. An astute Helen summarizes the situation.

Helen:

"Jimmy, are you saying that the seller is willing to carry a contract but wants more than twenty-five thousand down?"

Jimmy:

"Yes."

The cliff edge holds no further danger for Helen. She's moved away from it. The counteroffer is accepted.

Helen:

"I'd much rather have the house than the new furniture. We can always get new furniture later."

Harold:

"I thought that your heart was set on new furniture."

His pseudo-defense for the furniture is even weaker as he slips into the past-tense.

Helen:

"I thought your heart was set on getting it for me."

This was a win-win for everyone. The Homesteaders got the house they wanted without exceeding their available cash. Mr. Castle got his full price. Jimmy made a full-commission sale. His expert use of Cliffhangers caused success.

The next story reveals a situation in which someone at a crowded airport is trying to get a ride on a ten-passenger van into the city. The driver's ability to use a Cliffhanger properly has a positive effect on the outcome.

* * *

Crowded Van

The airport baggage area was crowded. Passengers from three different flights were retrieving their luggage at the same time. Waiting cars, taxis, buses and limos were queued up outside. Mike Mallis was in a hurry to get to his hotel where he was to attend a furniture convention. Carrying two suitcases and a carry-on bag, he rushed up to the van driver.

"I'm in a big hurry," he demanded. "Aren't you going downtown?"

"Yes. Get in. I'll put your bags in the back," replied the driver. "I'm scheduled to depart in twelve minutes."

"Can't we leave now? I'm in a hurry."

"I'm sorry, sir."

Mallis waited impatiently. As the minutes slowly passed, more passengers got in. The van was filling up quickly. Mallis glared at the elderly woman seated next to him...and then at his watch. "These drivers are all the same," he muttered. "They don't care if we're late."

After eleven minutes, the driver got in and started the engine. Suddenly, he heard a shrill whistle. An airline pilot waved from the terminal door. He was carrying a suitcase. Another pilot and two flight attendants followed him to the van. The driver got out and opened the door.

"Can we all fit?" asked the pilot.

"It'll be tight. We'll manage," replied the driver.

"We'll sit on your laps," said one of the flight attendants to the pilots.

"That might work," responded the driver.

They squeezed in. The van left on schedule.

Mallis was perspiring, his blood pressure rose. His ride to town in the airport van was miserable.

* * *

Let's see how the use of a Cliffhanger might have changed Mallis' disposition. We'll start the story over and alter the dialogue.

"I'm in a big hurry," demanded Mike Mallis. "Aren't you going downtown?"

"Yes," replied the driver, "but I'll be very crowded. Three planes are in. You'll enjoy the ride more on the next trip. More room."

There's the Cliffhanger. The driver knows that crowded vans make passengers unhappy, so he tells everybody that space will be limited. Most passengers would prefer to be crowded than not go. All can see the lineup of taxicabs waiting with lots of room for a faster, but more costly trip. The cliff is defined as not going in this van. To keep from falling off, Mallis has to accept the crowded conditions.

"When's the next trip?" asked Mallis.

"Forty-five minutes."

"I'll go with you." Mallis volunteers to be crowded.

"Okay, hop in. I'll put your bags aboard. It's going to crowded, though. Make yourself skinny. I'm leaving in twelve minutes."

"Thanks."

Mallis waited patiently. How lucky, he thought. He'd rather get there sooner than be comfortable...and not pay the extra cost of a taxicab. More passengers got in as the minutes passed rapidly. Mallis looked at the elderly woman seated next to him. "Have you got enough room? I can squeeze over a little bit."

"Thank you. You're very kind. I think I'm all right. She smiled at him.

After eleven minutes, the driver got in and started the engine. Suddenly he heard a shrill whistle. An airline pilot waved from the terminal door. He was carrying a suitcase. Another pilot and two flight attendants followed him to the van.

"There's some more people," Mallis called out to the driver. "Better wait!"

The driver got out and opened the door.

"Can we all fit?" asked the pilot.

"It'll be tight. We'll manage," replied the driver.

"We'll sit on your laps," said one of the flight attendants to the pilots.

Everybody laughed.

"Give me your suitcase," said Mallis. "I'll prop it up on my knees."

"That should work," responded the driver.

"Thanks, mister," said the pilot. "Where you come in from?"

"Denver."

They all got in. The crowded van left on schedule, with everyone talking congenially the whole way.

Using Cliffhangers properly requires practice and skill. Opportunities are ever present to practice this high profile sales tactic.

What are you thinking of?

Chapter Eight

The Ray Gun

The Long Voyage

It was the year 2327. Starship America, under the command of Commodore Starr, had just returned from a two hundred year mission into the outer galaxy. The bodies of the crew were frozen most of that time, so it was okay. The knowledge gained was formidable, and the scientific breakthroughs would have everlasting value to planet Earth. The debriefing for the entire expedition took less than one nanosecond. The reason? Commodore Starr had his Ray Gun. He aimed it at the debriefer's forehead, instantly, the debriefer had in his mind every detail of the entire journey.

Meanwhile, back in the twenty-first century, Jimmy Dover had perfected the use of a verbal version of the Ray Gun, another high profile sales tactic.

*   *   *

Trip to Europe Questions

The short little round man entered the showroom. "What can you tell me about leasing?"he asked Jimmy Dover, who had his Ray Gun handy.

"What's all what about leasing?" asked Jimmy. He recognized a Trip to Europe Question when he heard one.

"One of my co-workers leases his car. What can you tell me about it?"

Jimmy smiled. "It sounds like you'd like me to tell you in twenty-five words or less all about leasing. Is that right?"

"I guess so."

"Believe it or not, I have a twenty-five words or less explanation so that you can find out all about leasing. The problem with the human language is that to actually say twenty-five words takes about thirty seconds. Now, the question is, do you have thirty seconds so that I can tell you all about leasing?"

"I guess so."

* * *

A Trip to Europe question can be devastating. In fact, it's a waste of time for both parties. People's conversations are permeated with them. When one is asked, zero communication occurs. Many people have the mistaken belief that Trip to Europe Questions are buying questions.

To explain, let's relate what occurs when a person returns from a trip to Europe. For many, part of the enjoyment of going on a trip anywhere is returning home and telling their friends and co-workers about it. The problem is that their friends and co-workers aren't really interested. They didn't get to go. But since they're acquaintances, they act interested.

Let's listen in.

"How was your trip to Europe?" asks the acquaintance.

"Fabulous. Just fabulous. Our first day England, I went to Buckingham Palace and watched the palace guards. They don't ever smile. When we got there..."

"Sounds great." The acquaintance looks at his wristwatch. "Holy smokes, is it that late? I'm late for a meeting. Next time I see you, I'd like to hear all about it. Gotta run."

Exit the acquaintance. When he realized the reply to his initial question would go beyond two or three words, he fled.

The questioner would prefer the dialogue went as follows:

"How was your trip to Europe?"

"Fabulous. Just fabulous."

"That's great. Gotta go. I'm late for a meeting."

The problem with a Trip to Europe Question is that the questioner isn't interested. Many believe, however, that they are.

Another example:

An acquaintance spots Susan exiting the elevator.

"Good morning, Susan. How are you?"

"Sick as a dog. Stomach pains kept me up all night."

"Sorry to hear that. Goodbye now."

* * *

Programmed greetings and responses have no meaning. They're simply banal acknowledgments of our presence. How do you do? Fine. Keep your chin up. Thanks. How's everything? Not bad. How's little Timmy? They took him off the critical list last night. That's nice.

What if instead: How do you do? How do I do what? Keep your chin up. The Sistine Chapel is the only productive place to do that. How's everything. Everything includes my present condition and I'd like you to know all about it.

Those won't occur, of course. People don't expect literal answers to Trip to Europe Questions.

Wouldn't it be great if when you're asked a Trip to Europe Question, you could reach into a holster, pull out your Ray Gun, point it at the questioner's forehead, pull the trigger, and zap!! In a flash, you'd transmit every glorious nuance of your trip to Europe. The questioner would at once be filled with awe, appreciation, and complete understanding. Unfortunately, nobody has invented such a device, except in science fiction fantasies. Hence, you must create your own.

Examples of Trip to Europe Questions: What's the publishing business like? How do you like living in Poughkeepsie? What can you tell me about the Kiwanis Club? What's it like running a radio station? How was your family reunion last week? Why should I vote for Candidate Madison? The reader may be astonished at how frequently he's asked and asks Trip to Europe Questions.

Let's examine the dialogue between Jimmy and the Short Little Round Man.

* * *

Short Little Round Man:

"One of my co-workers leases his car. What can you tell me about it?"

Jimmy:

"It sounds like you'd like me to tell you in twenty-five words or less all about leasing. Is that right?"

Short Little Round Man:

"I guess so."

Jimmy:

"Believe it or not, I have a twenty-five words or less explanation so that you can find out all about leasing. The problem with the human language is that to actually say twenty-five words takes about thirty seconds. Now, the question is, do you have thirty seconds so that I can tell you all about leasing?"

Short Little Round Man:

"I guess so."

* * *

The prospect unreasonably expects Jimmy to give him complete insight into a complicated subject in less than five seconds. Jimmy has the burden of not knowing yet what will interest the prospect about the subject before he looks at his watch and flees the scene. Consequently,

Jimmy must create the time to use his Ray Gun and obtain the prospect's permission. Certainly more than five seconds will be required. Is it unreasonable to request thirty seconds? There's a possibility that the prospect is totally baffled, wondering how in the world he got into this, since he expected his rush tactic to get immediate information. If the prospect replies "no" to the thirty seconds request, he'll be blatantly rude. It's not polite to ask a question and then not allow time for an answer. Keep in mind...the prospect asked the first question!

* * *

Here's a ridiculous portrayal of the irony.

"May I ask you a question?"

"Of course. May I give you an answer?"

"No."

* * *

Jimmy now has the prospect's permission to take thirty seconds to explain leasing. It should be noted that Jimmy has already taken the better part of two minutes to reach this point, and the prospect hasn't yet looked at his watch. Now is the moment to pull out the Ray Gun.

Part of the fun of this tactic is you can do anything you choose during the thirty seconds...including doing nothing! You've obtained the prospect's permission! You can now turn into a character that will hopefully match up with the prospect. Remember that old television series, Gunsmoke, in which very little happened. Lots of drawls and pauses. Doc walked down the stairs from his second floor medical office muttering all the way; Matt complained about Chester's coffee in the jailhouse; Kitty sipped a drink at a card table in the Long Branch Saloon and said, "Hi" to Matt when he entered. The action during these character scenes may have been slow-paced, but what great characters they were, sustaining twenty years of tv Saturday nights. That, coincidentally, is one of the prize ingredients of a great salesperson...a great character.

* * *

Jimmy:

"Thank you. Well, let's see now. Thirty seconds isn't much time. But, oh well...oops. What's wrong with my watch? Oh wait. That can't be. Oh, I see. I need to look at the seconds hand. There. Let my thirty seconds begin now. Okay?"

Short Little Round Man:

"Sure thing."

Jimmy:

"Thanks again. First off, when you lease a vehicle, you can avoid the prepayment of sales tax, that's hundreds of dollars. You can avoid the prepayment of interest. That's hundreds of dollars. You can beat the government. You can beat the bank. You can beat the risk. You can beat inflation. You can sell your present vehicle and keep most of your equity in your savings account, since we don't need it for a big down payment. And your monthly payments will be fifteen, twenty, twenty-five dollars less...even more per month, depending on everything."

Jimmy's demeanor has changed. He set up the Ray Gun perfectly by getting the prospect's permission, then held his attention by fumbling with his watch, and increased the prospect's desire for Jimmy to get on with it. Then, like machine gun bullets pouring out of his Ray Gun, Jimmy let loose with a barrage of good reasons to lease. All were ways the prospect could spend less money! One benefit after another rained on the prospect. And Jimmy, like a chameleon, changed from the country bumpkin to the knowledgeable lease expert, though he continued to speak at the same tone and pace.

Jimmy:

"Well, my thirty seconds are up. So, I guess you can get going if you like."

Short Little Round Man:

"What do you mean, I can beat the government?"

Finally!! A Buying Question!!!

The prospect could have asked any number of different questions at this point. For example, "Did you say I could avoid the prepayment of interest?" or "How can I beat the bank?" He could even have terminated the conversation, but now he knows something that interests him.

It's possible that the prospect knew so little about the subject that he didn't know what to ask initially. It should be noted that the Ray Gun is effective only when the salesperson knows the product or service well. Jimmy didn't stumble or mumble when the bullets blazed out of the Ray Gun.

*   *   *

Mystifying Statements

Mary has just come over to Joann's house to see if she'll watch her five year old daughter while she goes shopping. When Mary gets there, Joann shows her one of her projects.

Mary:

"You're making the quilt for your church bazaar?"

Joann:

"It's not just any bazaar. There's something special about this one."

Mary:

"What's that?"

Mary begins with a Trip to Europe Question. Joann's skillful reply requires Mary to ask a second question. Mary doesn't know that Joann has promised her church that she'd invite every family on her block.

Joann:

"Sharing. Caring. Hundreds of people helping others in our city. Thousands of dollars are at stake. Everyone who helps can earn hundreds of dollars.

A Mystifying Statement!

Mary:

"How does one profit from a charity?"

The Trip to Europe Question has been replaced with a buying question caused by Joann's use of Mystifying Statements. Joann used her Ray Gun. The bullets were charity, money, earn hundreds of dollars, and the fact that everybody will be involved.

Joann:

"Have you looked in your garage lately? I mean really looked. Or in your attic?"

Another Mystifying Statement! Mary can't terminate the conversation without being rude. Who is in control? Is Joann a good advocate for the church project? She'll inform Mary that this is her golden opportunity to get rid of her rummage. The church will pay her twenty-five percent of the proceeds from her unwanteds. Everyone will benefit. The church will even send over a truck to pick it up.

Joann could have been a plain Jane, handling this situation in a routine manner, sparking zero interest from Mary, and accomplishing nothing. Without Mystifying Statements, the dialogue might have been as follows:

Mary:

"You're making the quilt for your church bazaar?"

Joann:

"That's right, Mary. Why don't you plan to come?"

Mary:

"Gosh, Joann, I don't know. When is it?"

Joann:

"A week from Saturday."

Mary:

"Let me check with Herb. See what he has planned. I think we might already have something scheduled for that day."

In this dialogue, there's no opportunity for Mary to discover any reason to participate. Joann mentioned only the bazaar. Zero benefits for Mary. The Ray Gun and Mystifying Statements are unused.

Trip to Europe Questions occur dozens of times daily. Often they're the epitome of insincerity. After all, when an acquaintance asks how you're feeling...then doesn't listen to your answer...how sincere can he be? We'll test this in the next situation.

*　　　*　　　*

Plastic Bucket

The telephone in Jimmy Dover's office rang. He picked up.

"Jimmy? This is Charlie Rogers with KPUK Radio. How are you today?"

"Not so good, Charlie. This morning when I got up, I was dizzy and felt sick to my stomach. My wife wanted me to stay home, but I couldn't. So she insisted that I bring a little Plastic Bucket to the office with me. It's sitting right next to my chair in case I throw up. I've had a couple of close calls already. The phone startled me."

"Sorry to hear that. Listen. Your company can sponsor the World Series on my station. We have a special deal that will allow you to..."

Does Charlie care how Jimmy feels? No. He asked a Trip to Europe Question and couldn't care less about Jimmy's reply. He cares only about discussing his own business. If you were Jimmy, would you choose to do business with Charlie?

A more appropriate response from Charlie could have been, "Oh no, Jimmy! I hope you're not getting the flu. It's going around. Everyone knows what a workhorse you are. You need to care about yourself more than your business. I'll call you back when you're feeling better."

At this point, Jimmy could accept Charlie's offer to call back or ask him why he's calling. Chances are better for the latter, because Charlie would have shown empathy about Jimmy's illness and complimented his work ethic.

"That's okay, Charlie. I feel good enough to talk to you right now. What's on your mind?"

The Ray Gun, Mystifying Statements, and the Plastic Bucket are invaluable high profile tactics that neutralize Trip to Europe Questions.

In the next story, Jimmy has what he believes is a great idea. He wants to try it out on the president of a big corporation. Layers of management permeate large companies. They serve to screen ideas from the decision makers. Jimmy knows that only one person can say "yes" to an idea. The president. Jimmy utilizes all his resources on Mr. Big.

* * *

Big Opportunity

Jimmy Dover sat alone in the boardroom of the supermarket chain waiting for the meeting to begin. The company's president had agreed to see him at ten o'clock. Five more minutes. Jimmy stared at his reflection in the highly-polished boardroom table. Sixteen elegantly upholstered leather chairs surrounded the long table. Jimmy wondered which end of the table was Mr. Big's. It occurred to Jimmy that Mr. Big might even sit in the middle of one side, just like he'd seen in news photos of the U.S. President presiding over Cabinet meetings.

Two days earlier, Jimmy had phoned Mr. Big and informed him that he was a business consultant with absolutely no knowledge or experience in the grocery business, and that he worked with several hundred clients throughout the United States, Canada and Australia. Jimmy had gone on to say that several days earlier, while sitting on an airplane, he'd been struck by a startling revelation about how to deal better with supermarket customers and get more favorable attention for the grocery chain.

"In any event," said Jimmy, "if you share my enthusiasm, you'll be able to do so in about twenty minutes. I wouldn't plan to take up your whole day. If it's not a good idea, well, then I'll learn something, too. And I'll simply leave quietly."

In one paragraph, Jimmy employed several high profile sales tactics including Guts to Fail, Pulling the String, and Ray Gun Bullets.

"If by accident I do have a good idea" he continued, "then you can invite me to stay longer if you like."

"I'm always open to new ideas," replied Mr. Big. "Sometimes the best ones come from outside the organization. If you'd like to come in next Wednesday morning at ten o'clock, I'd be happy to meet with you."

Jimmy looked at his watch. It was nine fifty-nine a.m. The door opened. Mr. Big entered.

"I hope I didn't keep you waiting, Mr. Dover. I just got out of another meeting." He introduced himself to Jimmy, then sat down next to him.

"About how much time do you need, Mr. Dover?" he asked. "I'll let my secretary know."

This impressed Jimmy. True decision-makers have a lot of class.

"Thanks for seeing me, Mr. Big," said Jimmy. "I really appreciate it. As I promised you on the phone last Monday, you'll know in twenty minutes or so if you aren't enthusiastic about what I have to say…and I was serious. If you aren't doing a tap dance on the table within twenty minutes, I'll leave quietly. Do you have that much time?"

"Take whatever time you need. Would you care for some coffee or a soft drink?"

"No thank you."

Mr. Big picked up the telephone. "Ruth, come in here for a minute?"

Seconds later, she entered.

"Ruth, I believe you've met Mr. Dover. Bring us a pot of coffee and anything he'd like."

The Ray Gun bullets Jimmy used two days earlier were 1. dealing better with supermarket customers; 2. getting more favorable attention for the grocery chain; 3. Jimmy's experience with clients all over the world; and 4. a startling revelation he couldn't get out of his mind. The first sounded specific, but was only general. All were subjects that company presidents are always concerned about. Salespeople who are too specific when introducing particular benefits are often not believed. They're dismissed with a terse, "We already have a program that addresses that subject," or "I believe that our Mr. Small could be helpful with you on that. I suggest you contact him."

Naturally, if Jimmy can meet and talk to Mr. Big, why would he settle for Mr. Small, who has plenty of authority to say no, but zero authority to say yes? Most of the Mr. Smalls of this world are afraid to take the responsibility…and certainly don't have the authority.

Besides using the Ray Gun, Jimmy revealed his Guts to Fail. He volunteered that within twenty minutes, Mr. Big would recognize whether or not he liked the idea. Jimmy acknowledged the possibility that his idea might not have merit. Mr. Big tested him immediately. Many salespeople promise in advance that their presentations will require only ten minutes…or whatever…but hope to take two hours. When Jimmy reminded Mr. Big of his twenty minute promise, Mr. Big began to believe that he might just like the idea, because Jimmy was an honorable person. To assure that Jimmy wouldn't rush through his presentation, Mr. Big relaxed the conditions somewhat by offering a drink. Jimmy still didn't back down from his time commitment...as he initially rejected the drink offer. Mr. Big responded by ordering drinks anyway. An early buying signal. He liked Jimmy, wanted him to stay, and wanted to like his presentation. He'd known Jimmy for less than three minutes.

Now was the time for Jimmy to Pull the String and prepare for a second use of the Ray Gun, so that before twenty minutes had elapsed, Mr. Big would know for certain that he wanted to like the idea.

"Before I begin," said Jimmy, "I want to remind you that I have no experience in the supermarket business, and the fact that I'm here today is the result of a fluky accident that happened to me on the airplane the other day. That's when I called you. After the plane landed, of course."

Mr. Big was glued to his chair. He looked like he appreciated Jimmy's candor, and that he didn't come across like some New York City hotshot, but instead like a country bumpkin with knowledge and know-how...a cross between Columbo and Gomer Pyle...or possibly Will Rogers and Jimmy Stewart.

"Anyway," said Jimmy, "let me take up the first two minutes of my twenty minutes to offer a comment about your business. I've already said that I could be absolutely dead wrong. But, if I am, then there's no need for me to get into my idea, because it's so dependent on your favorable response to my comment."

A Cliffhanger! Jimmy squirmed in his chair as though there were a high probability that Mr. Big would have an unfavorable response. Ruth returned with a pot of coffee and two glasses of Dr. Pepper.

"Don't worry about the time, Jimmy," said Mr. Big, as he reached out for the string. "Take whatever you need. Thank you, Ruth. Hold my calls. Oh, and would you let Mr. Small know I can't meet with him until late this afternoon. Have him check with you again right after lunch."

Ruth smiled at Jimmy and exited. Mr. Big had eradicated the time restriction. Jimmy had not even begun his presentation.

"Thanks again for your kind courtesy," said Jimmy. "When I was on that airplane a couple of days ago, I was thinking about the economy, about a possible recession, about the unemployment rate, about the President's speech last week on television; and I thought to myself, 'if the general economy gets bad, if business slows down somewhat, if we actually do have something worse than a mild recession and slide into a depression, what business can withstand it?' I thought to myself right then and there, the depression-proof business of businesses is the supermarket business. I determined that I needed to come up with a viable program for a supermarket chain. So, before the plane landed, I came up with what I believe is an exciting concept for the grocery business. I opened up the phone book at the airport, called you. Here I am. Are you ready?"

Mr. Big topped off his coffee. "Yes, I'd like to hear this idea of yours."

Jimmy knew it would have been impossible for Mr. Big to terminate the meeting at this point. Even though he showed subtle signs of excitement about hearing Jimmy's idea, outwardly he exhibited calm. Wouldn't it be tremendous if one could affix electrocardiogram electrodes to a prospect's body in order to measure his level of excitement? A cardiac surgeon could probably qualify as a psychiatrist just by having his patients' electrocardiogram tapes to look at during the interview.

"This is the basic premise, Mr. Big. This is the part you'll have to agree to at the outset if my idea is to have any merit at all." (Another Cliffhanger).

Jimmy took two big swallows from his Dr. Pepper. Mr. Big waited.

"When you advertise products in your weekly grocery ads," said Jimmy, "I believe that most of the shoppers think that you are advertising the items that you want to sell…not the items that they necessarily want to buy. I realize that is not true, Mr. Big. You go to a lot of trouble each week to assure that the items you put in your newspaper ads are the items your customers want to buy most; but I submit that most of your customers don't know that. They believe instead that the items they see advertised are the ones you want to sell. Would you say that was true, Mr. Big?"

"Yes. From the customer's point of view."

"That's what I've always thought. So, when you're featuring Starbucks Coffee or Pillsbury cake mix in your weekly ads, your customers believe that you want to sell Starbucks Coffee or Pillsbury cake mix; you're not necessarily featuring those items because your customers want to buy those particular products. And, they believe that you're making a lot of profit on it...or you have some left over stock you need to get rid of. Many have no concept that you bring in railroad cars full of it for the sale."

Mr. Big gazed at Jimmy with curious interest. He admitted later he'd never heard his advertising manager or marketing staff say anything like this, and that he was almost afraid to reply for fear that Jimmy's unstated idea would be lost or left unsaid.

"Now, we both know that's not true," said Jimmy. "You go to a tremendous amount of effort to feature those items that will appeal to the most customers. And, contrary to making profit, they're usually loss-leaders."

So far, Jimmy knew he'd not told Mr. Big anything that he didn't already know, But, Jimmy was demonstrating that he knew a lot about general merchandising, and he was using this knowledge to set up the Ray Gun, so that when he finally stated his idea, it would be a solution to a problem that already existed in the grocery business and was acknowledged by Mr. Big. Ironically, in this case, Mr. Big and others in his position never realized this was a problem

"Here's my idea, Mr. Big. Are you ready?"

"I'm ready."

Mr. Big fidgeted in his chair as though searching for the right mix of ennui and attention.

"Before I tell you what it is, let me ask you a question first. Would you mind if I asked a question?"

"What is it?"

When Jimmy finally unveils his idea, Mr. Big will have fought off a huge desire to choke it out of him. Consider the alternative to this conversation. Jimmy could have come in a few minutes earlier, acted like a pompous, big shot who knew everything about the supermarket business, and briefly outlined the idea. The alienated Mr. Big would most likely have shown him the door within five minutes...even though he committed to ten. But Jimmy followed the principles of high profile sales tactics. In the same way that asking someone to try not to think of an orange...and rendering him unable to get it out of his mind...so has Jimmy's undisclosed idea been tantalizingly swung before the prospect's eyes, just out of his reach, causing him to consciously consider sitting on his hands to keep from lunging at it like a crazed kitten.

The moment has arrived to unholster his Ray Gun.

"Well, here's the question," said Jimmy. "What if through your advertising from now on...yes, this is a good way to ask this. Mr. Big, what if through your advertising from now on you could demonstrate that your customers believed you were advertising what they wanted to buy, not what you wanted to sell? Would there be any merit to your supermarket chain if you could get them to believe that?"

Mr. Big leaned across his desk unable to control his facial expression. "Can you do that?"

Jimmy looked down sheepishly at the floor. He squirmed as though uncomfortable. He looked like the reincarnation of Will Rogers.

"I'm not sure," he said in a quiet voice. "But, that's what I came here to talk with you about. And, after I explain several possible approaches, you'll be able to make your own value judgment about it. However, I'm not aware of anyone who has ever done this before. So, in some respects, you'll be pioneering something new in the supermarket business that nobody's ever done before. If you have any qualms about being a pioneer, Mr. Big, you could tell me now so that I won't waste any of your time."

The foregoing is a clear example of the effect of utilizing several high profile tactics in tandem. If Mr. Big were asked afterward to try not to think of Jimmy Dover...how could he not? The Ray Gun was brought out at the moment of maximum desire, and the benefits of Jimmy's ideas were readily accepted by Mr. Big, before he even heard the idea.

Let's analyze the conversation.

* * *

Mr. Big:

"About how much time do you need, Mr. Dover? I'll let my secretary know."

He's testing Jimmy's earlier promise to take only twenty minutes.

Jimmy:

"Thanks for seeing me, Mr. Big. I really appreciate it. As I promised you on the phone last Monday, you'll know in twenty minutes or so if you aren't enthusiastic about what I want to say...and I was serious. If you aren't doing a tap dance on the table within twenty minutes, I'll leave quietly. Do you have that much time?"

Mr. Big:

"Take whatever time you need. Would you care for some coffee or a soft drink?"

This is a mild buying signal. The prospect wants Jimmy to take longer than twenty minutes, because he wants to like his idea. He likes him. Jimmy passed his preliminary test.

Jimmy:

"No thank you."

Mr. Big dangled the yarn in front of him, but Jimmy didn't reach out for it. He's honoring his earlier promise and not agreeing to anything that will lengthen the time.

Mr. Big:

"Ruth, come in here for a minute?

He's aggressively making his own arrangements to lengthen the time.

Mr. Big:

"Ruth, I believe you've met Mr. Dover. Bring us a pot of coffee and anything he'd like."

Jimmy:

"Before I begin, I want to remind you that I have no experience in the supermarket business, and the fact that I'm here today is the result of a fluky accident that happened to me on the airplane the other day. That's when I called you. After the plane landed, of course."

This is a reverse. Extensive research, planning, and money do not necessarily guarantee success. Remember the Edsel? What about Lofty Platitudes? Jimmy's avoiding them...just as he should to eliminate negative responses.

Jimmy:

"Anyway, let me take up the first two minutes of my twenty minutes to make a comment about your business, a personal opinion. I've already said that I could be absolutely dead wrong. But, if I am, then there's no need for me to get into my idea, because my whole idea depends on your favorable response to my comment."

Standing on the edge of the cliff, Mr. Big must give the right answer for Jimmy to continue. It's much easier to extend the time with a prospect by obtaining his permission. The alternative is to drone on interminably without it and irritate the prospect into cutting off the salesperson in mid-presentation.

Mr. Big:

"Don't worry about the time, Jimmy. Take whatever you need. Thank you, Ruth. Hold my calls."

For the second time, he's working to extend the time. He wants to make certain that Jimmy explains his idea properly. Mr. Big has bought something. Jimmy Dover.

Mr. Big:

"Oh, and would you let Mr. Small know I can't meet with him until late this afternoon. Have him check with you again right after lunch."

See how little authority Mr. Small has? Even Ruth has power over him.

Jimmy:

"Thanks again for your kind courtesy. When I was on that airplane a couple of days ago, I was thinking about the economy, about a possible recession, about the unemployment rate, about the President's speech last week on television..."

Mystifying Statements pervade. All are about subjects that many company leaders are concerned about. Middle managers are usually focused on their assignments, and if Jimmy were talking with one, he'd use a different approach. But company leaders are concerned with the big picture. Many, in fact, lay awake nights hoping for insight and inspiration.

Jimmy:

"...and I thought to myself, 'if the general economy gets bad, if business slows down somewhat, if we actually do have something worse than a mild recession and slide into a depression, what business can withstand it?'

The prospect might be wishing he was tape recording this for material for his next stockholders meeting.

Jimmy:

"I thought to myself right then and there, the depression-proof business of businesses is the supermarket business. I determined that I needed to come up with a viable program for a supermarket chain."

Mr. Big believes that Jimmy is smart enough to do whatever he wishes. He needs only a good enough reason. If the reason is unexpected or accidental, so much the better. Many companies have many warm bodies sitting around headquarters charged with the responsibility of creating solutions to problems and opportunities. Oft times they don't. Perhaps Jimmy, with no knowledge of the grocery business and therefore no preconceived roadblocks or biases, will.

Jimmy:

"So, before the plane landed, I came up with what I believe is an exciting concept for the grocery business. I opened up the phone book at the airport, called you. Here I am. Are you ready?"

Mr. Big:

"Yes, I'd like to hear this idea of yours."

Of course he's ready. But Jimmy doesn't want to take any chances about the prospect yearning to know the idea...so he reinforces the yearning. The prospect needs to be a good actor, though, to maintain a look of disinterest. It's difficult.

Jimmy:

"This is the basic premise, Mr. Big. This is the part you'll have to agree to at the outset if my idea is to have any merit at all."

Another Cliffhanger for the prospect! He's hanging upside down with his ankles wrapped around a twig that's breaking loose from the soil. This statement requires Mr. Big to show enthusiasm when Jimmy reveals his basic premise. If he doesn't, Jimmy will leave without telling him the idea.

Jimmy:

"When you advertise products in your weekly grocery ads, I believe that most of the shoppers think that you are advertising the items that you want to sell...not the items that they necessarily want to buy. I realize that is not true, Mr. Big. You go to a lot of trouble each week to assure that the items you put in your newspaper ads are the items your customers want to buy most; but I submit that most of your customers don't know that. They believe instead that the items they see advertised are the ones you want to sell. Would you say that was true, Mr. Big?"

Mr. Big:

"Yes. From the customer's point of view."

Jimmy:

"That's what I've always thought. So, when you're featuring Starbucks Coffee or Pillsbury cake mix in your weekly ads, your customers believe that you want to sell Starbucks Coffee or Pillsbury cake mix; you're not necessarily featuring those items because your customers want to buy those particular products. And, they believe that you're making a lot of profit on it...or you have some left over stock you need to get rid of. Many have no concept that you bring in railroad cars full of it for the sale."

These are the Ray Gun Bullets for Jimmy's basic premise. He could have said all this a couple of days earlier, but the prospect would probably have wondered, 'Who is this guy? What does he know? What's he doing telling me my business? Why haven't I ever heard of him if he's so smart? Why doesn't he see my advertising manager? Why doesn't he leave me alone?' Now, however, the Ray Gun Bullets are very effective, because in preparing the proper climate for his presentation, Jimmy has caused Mr. Big to reach out for the ball of yarn, utilized his Guts to Fail, included some Mystifying Statements, and prefaced everything with a Cliffhanger. Jimmy has made the Ray Gun a powerful weapon!

Jimmy:

"Here's my idea, Mr. Big. Are you ready?"

Mr. Big:

"I'm ready."

Jimmy takes nothing for granted. He continues to volunteer to stop at any time by obtaining the prospect's permission to proceed. He didn't need to ask him outright whether he accepted the basic premise. He simply asked if he's ready.

Jimmy:

"Before I tell you what it is, let me ask you a question first. Would you mind if I asked a question?"

Mr. Big:

"What is it?"

Jimmy:

"Well, here's the question. What if through your advertising from now on...yes, this is a good way to ask this. Mr. Big, what if through your advertising from now on you could demonstrate that your customers believed you were advertising what they wanted to buy, not what you wanted to sell? Would there be any merit to your supermarket chain if you could get them to believe that?"

Jimmy has nailed down the basic premise, and now he's establishing that his approach is needed by Mr. Big. If a prospect doesn't need a service or product, he certainly won't buy it, will he?

Mr. Big:

"Can you do that?"

Victory! Jimmy knows that he can now take all day to express his idea if needed. What if Jimmy had stated his idea when he'd first arrived? It's possible and probable that Mr. Big would have responded with something like 'We already do advertise what our customer want to buy. We go to a lot of trouble to accomplish that. If that's your idea, I'm afraid it's not original. We're already doing that. But, thanks for coming in.'

Of course, Jimmy handled it differently. He waited until he knew Mr. Big wanted to like the idea and was practically begging to hear it. Then, Jimmy pulled out his Ray Run, pointed it at Mr. Big's forehead, and pulled the trigger.

What if the idea isn't any good? Apply that question to yourself, dear reader. Suppose an idea you're working on isn't any good? Why, then, continue to work on it? Can anyone effectively work on a project, represent a product or service, participate in a campaign, embrace an idea that he believes is no good? And even when you believe in and know the worth of a project or idea, you cannot have the best chance to sell it to someone until you first set up the proper circumstances for the prospect to want to take the proper time to learn about it, to want to like it, and to already like and trust you. Many grand ideas go unused and turn to dust because of poor presentations. Many brilliant solutions are untried due to improper expression.

In practiced hands, the Ray Gun is a potent weapon.

By the way, what are you thinking of?

Chapter Nine

Star Quality

People with Star Quality cause others to buy tickets to watch them perform. Charisma has a similar meaning. Everyone can develop Star Quality, though, even when charisma may be lacking.

Charismatic Performers

Think about those who are written about in history books...the politicians, inventors, social reformers, dictators, military figures, criminals, entertainers, crackpots, futurists, freaks, heroes, cowards and misfits. What makes them so special? Star Quality represents a quirkiness, difference, and uniqueness...and it's something all of us can emulate to break out of the mold of the average person. Even though some charismatic performers may be flukes, most have attributes that set them apart.

Developing our talents requires great effort. Then, to get favorable attention we need to take on characteristics, peculiarities, and methods of expression that cause us to stand out. Audiences love a good performance and pay big bucks, in the same way a buyer rewards the successful seller for effective persuasion. To quote Shakespeare, "All the world's a stage, and all the men and women merely players." It's acting! The resulting persona enhances your likability, believability, and irresistibility. When the curtain is up, all eyes are on you.

Achievers know that life is a stage, and that outstanding success requires a bravo performance. When we consider the famous and infamous of the past or present, it makes no difference whether they're real or fictional, because their images are firmly etched. General Douglas MacArthur,

Robin Hood, Winston Churchill, Citizen Kane, John Wayne, Lucille Ball, Inspector Clousseau, Jesse James, Snow White, Ronald Reagan, Madeleine Kahn, Columbo, Babe Ruth, Lee Iacocca, Walter Mitty, Clint Eastwood, Seinfeld, Woody Allen, Gandhi, Don Knotts, McCloud, Bette Davis, Jay Leno, Butch Cassidy, Shirley Temple, General Custer, Orphan Annie, Charlie Brown...the list goes on and on.

*　　　*　　　*

Role-Playing

Star Quality involves role-playing by taking on characteristics, mannerisms, and affectations of others that are compatible with our own personalities. It also involves doing the unexpected.

Think about a family that belongs to your church, parish, or synagogue, for example, wearing their Sunday clothes and appealing social manners as they sit in the pew during the service. What were they like two hours earlier, though, when mom was preparing breakfast, getting the baby bathed, and shaking dad out of bed, while the teenagers argued about using the bathroom. Do they act differently at home than they do at church? Or at school or at work or during an IRS audit or in a long line at the grocery store or with the school counselor or at a city council meeting? We're all chameleons. Role-playing is a part of everyone's life.

A prospect at an automobile dealership may expect the salesperson he meets to correspond to a preconceived image, which may not be flattering. Suppose, instead he meets a salesperson who is caring, amiable, easy going, and charming. Would that be disconcerting and unexpected? And possibly rewarding and memorable?

If a borrower expects the loan officer at the bank to bc haughty, strict, and stuffy, won't he be surprised and slowed down when he meets one who is down-home, vulnerable, and concerned? Those characteristics may be so disarming that the loan applicant will lower his guard and reveal more of his true self. It's two-sided.

If a person turns people off by being a stuffed-shirt, then he must develop Star Quality to eliminate that aspect of his personality and demeanor. On the other hand, if he's a soft touch, then he must project some steely qualities to offset that weakness.

* * *

Matching Up

There's a Dr. Jekyll and Mr. Hyde in all of us...not necessarily a split personality, good versus evil, competent versus incompetent, responsible versus frivolous; but instead more like inhibited versus role-playing Steve Martin, or unassuming versus role playing Julie Roberts, or unaggressive versus role playing Carol Burnett, or suave and debonair versus role playing Billy Crystal or Tim Allen, or well-prepared versus role playing Columbo or Gomer Pyle.

Imagine your banker replacing Jay Leno in a television special, or the supermarket checker standing in for Katy Couric. Conjure up your mail carrier replacing Michael J. Fox or Tom Cruise, and your next door neighbor emulating Regis Philbin or Bruce Willis.

Would anyone pay money to watch? Many people are without charisma...that magic something that attracts ticket buyers. Most of us have our families, co-workers, neighbors, circle of friends...and when we die, then a funeral, a classified obituary, and an R.I.P. on the grave marker. There's no testimonial on television, no annual tribute. Only memories and photos and family lore remain. Some say they're satisfied with the mundane. There's an alternative. It's called Matching Up.

What is it about you, dear reader, that when people meet you for the first time causes them to want to stay with you rather than flee? In a selling situation, the salesperson must be slightly below the prospect at all times...in temperament, ability, education, smarts, demeanor. At no time during the sales process can the prospect believe that the salesperson can outsmart him, or make any money off of him. If that occurs, the prospect will be thinking of only one thing...leaving. One's ability to stay slightly below the prospect at all times during the relationship is called Matching Up.

It's difficult to master. This is why. If you accept the premise that everyone you meet is different, but you act the same with each of them, you'll overmatch at least half the people you meet. Your seeming superiority will scare them off. To Match Up properly, you must be just slightly below the prospect...not a lot below or you'll come across as just plain stupid. Hence, you've got to alter your persona to be just below the prospect's level...and each prospect's level is different. Judgment is required to measure it.

An acquaintance worked full time for several years as a pool hustler. He had a lifestyle similar to that portrayed by the actor, Paul Newman, in the movie, "The Hustler", in 1962, and reprised in "The Color of Money" in 1986 as Fast Eddie. He traveled throughout the country playing high stakes pool matches. He made a good living. If you were challenged to identify him in a lineup of twenty people, you'd probably not succeed, because he doesn't look like what many believe a pool hustler looks like. My acquaintance looked like Huckleberry Finn...harmless-looking, innocent, naive. He even walked with a hobble. His opponents underestimated him. Some laughed openly when they met him. That was a large cause of his success. He'd mastered Matching Up. Moments before a match began, if he matched up properly, he'd win, even though his opponent was a better player.

In "The Hustler", Fast Eddie's goal was to beat Minnesota Fats (portrayed by Jackie Gleason). Eddie was shown to be a better player, but

Minnesota Fats won the match, because he matched up better. Eddie got drunk. Fats only drank juice. Eddie got tired. Fats spruced up every hour and conserved his energy. Eddie made excuses about the playing conditions. Fats felt right at home. Eddie acted like a loser. Fats looked like a winner. Eddie lost. Fats won...even though his opponent was a better player.

It's not enough to Match Up properly at the outset of a meeting, then take it for granted. The Match Up must be maintained throughout the entire get-together. So many salespeople Match Up at the beginning of the sales process, just long enough for them to feel comfortable with the prospect and the situation, then overmatch. A zero outcome results. The salesperson lets his personal comfort with the situation and prospect overwhelm his judgment. He becomes too glib or too smooth or too smart or too relaxed and resorts to mannerisms and speechifying that turns off the prospect such as putting his feet up on the desk or using a profanity or ignoring someone in the group or sounding greedy or uncaring or without empathy or taking something for granted or any hundreds of things that can cause the situation to go haywire.

We're all different. Each of us acts differently with each person we meet. Think about yourself, dear reader. Aren't you different with people who owe you money than you are with people you owe money to? And with employees than with employers? And with the loan officer at the bank than with the clerk at the hardware store? And with your child's teacher than you are with your child's playmate? And with the meter maid than with the mailman?

Why? Are you schizophrenic?

Of course not! Matching Up is a requirement we need to cope in our daily lives. Just like chameleons, whose colors change with the environment, our personae changes with each individual we meet so that we can communicate and relate to them at their own level of understanding.

*　　　*　　　*

Human Frailties

What is it that separates an appealing person from a stuffed shirt? Human frailties! Carve that in a rock! Vulnerability is a much-desired human trait. Is Columbo perfect? Does he act like he knows everything? No. He appears to have human frailties. Is Gomer Pyle perfect? No, because he has vulnerability.

Does Carol Burnett project perfection? No. She projects human frailties. What about Don Knott's character on the Andy Griffith Show? He acts like he thinks he's perfect, and the audience knows he's not. That's the role of Barney Fife...the know-it-all. All of the aforementioned were created to convey human frailties. They're planned and programmed vulnerability.

Pick a role. Choose a character. It makes no difference whether your choice is real or fictional. Go ahead and think of twenty thousand cops on the New York City Police Department; but there's one who is memorable...McCloud. Even though he's a fictional character played by the actor, Dennis Weaver, the fact remains that the character causes one cop to stand out among thousands...and a huge audience likes him. What about Andy Sipowicz on NYPD Blue? Or Diane on the same show? In a world of sameness, blandness, and anonymity, Star Quality is required. If the real you is no star, then the simple solution is to take on the Star Quality of others, copy their mannerisms, and stand out from those around you.

Of the billions of human beings who have populated planet Earth, very few are immortalized. But, those who are have a few things in common. Eccentricity, Guts to Fail, uniqueness. There have been thousands of military generals, and all but a few are long forgotten. General George Patton, with his pearl-handled revolvers and Guts to Fail, certainly stands out. As does Dwight D. Eisenhower, with his laid back, mellow demeanor. And Colin Powell. Would you buy a used car from him?

Most people strive for anonymity, thus the competition for Star Quality is practically nil. Role playing doesn't require the personality of an extrovert. Some of the most famous actors have been complete introverts...such as Henry Fonda and

Laurence Olivier and Carol Burnett and Johnny Carson. But, when they got to put on a mask, go on stage, and be somebody else, they shined. Their roles were masks behind which they could hide and perform freely without inhibition.

Jimmy Dover knows about role playing. He puts people at ease, entertains them, and at once encourages them to expose their true feelings. He deals with people at their own level of understanding and creates the proper mood to hold their attention. When the challenge goes out to try not to think of Jimmy Dover, he turns into an orange.

Let's review all the characters we've met in this book who have come under the spell of the high profile tactics that Jimmy utilized to meet their needs and accomplish his goals.

* * *

Curtain Call

Cast of Characters

Airline Ticket Agent

He couldn't make his company's Lofty Platitude advertising work until Jimmy showed him how.

Alice

She made Fred realize how much he loved her after she Pulled the String.

Barry Berry

He wanted to Pull the String and actually had it in his grasp for awhile.

Mr. Big

The Mr. Bigs of this world love good ideas and are receptive to changing the status quo when they are approached with high profile tactics.

Mr. Blatz

This Buick dealer didn't want Jimmy to get lost, because his Theater of the Mind had become 3D and Technicolor.

Mr. Blatz' Receptionist

Her training didn't prepare her for Jimmy Dover's high profile tactics.

Billy Bologne

He needed to learn how to avoid Lofty Platitudes.

Mr. Castle

He got his asking price for the house, because his agent employed Cliffhangers.

Venus Cauldron

FBI Interrogation School Questions work in singles bars, too.

Concrete Company Employee

Nobody ever asked him about his company's logo, because it wasn't an Arresting Trademark.

Jimmy Dover

Trying not to think of the book's protagonist is as difficult as trying not to think of an orange.

Felicity Fox

The bachelor's questioning technique prompted her forthrightness in the singles bar. She couldn't resist responding to FBI Interrogation School Questions.

Keenan & Mary Fawcett

They came face-to face with Non-Negotiable Factors when they opted to remodel their kitchen.

Fred

He discovered his love for Alice only after she Pulled the String.

Arthur Goodsell

He learned about Asking For a Turndown before the sales meeting.

Gloria Goodshape

She finally bought the dress after Jimmy Pulled the String.

Mr. Gray

This school supplies buyer realized he wouldn't buy the competitor's products…The Fifth W was missing.

Mrs. Guardian

Mr. Principal's secretary was enthralled by the Head of Lettuce and The Fifth W.

Harold & Helen Homesteader

They bought their dream house after some perilous Cliffhangers.

Joann

She employed Mystifying Statements for the church bazaar.

Mr. & Mrs. Johnson

They discovered that Non-Negotiable Factors such as inflation and government regulations drive up prices.

Kitten

The yarn it can't reach is what it desires most.

Little Boy

He learned about Pulling the String naturally...nobody told him about it.

Mary

She couldn't avoid Joann's Mystifying Statements about the bazaar.

Mike Mallis

His negative qualities were neutralized with high profile tactics in tandem.

Miss Counter

Theater of the Mind turned the tables on this devious telephone solicitor.

Percy

This plumber sprinkled Non-Negotiable Factors into his bids.

Doyle Peterson

He set up a challenging sales meeting by knowing that Asking For a Turndown would Pull the String.

Mr. Principal

He couldn't resist The Fifth W and the Head of Lettuce.

Restaurant Chain President

A fish story and the presence of several obvious flaws encouraged him to seek the positive in Jimmy, who pricked his Lofty Platitude introduction with a pin.

Charlie Rogers

He asked a Trip to Europe question, ignored the Plastic Bucket, and failed to make a sale.

Mr. Rush

He rushed into a Lofty Platitude, then Jimmy Pulled the String.

Short Little Round Man

His Trip to Europe Question became the target for the Ray Gun.

Mr. Small

Since he can't say yes, only no, why bother to talk to him?

Commodore Starr

He's got using the Ray Gun down to a science.

Steve Stroker

His feigned indifference was reversed by Pulling the String . There are a lot of strokers in this world.

Susan

Jimmy Dover's wife and sales trip companion was an eye witness to the practice of high profile tactics.

Uncle George

He viewed the remodeled family room in a new light after Harriet Pulled the String.

Mr. Wormwood

Hula hoops are nothing compared to Rap Wraps and toilet paper.

* * *

Employ high profile tactics and discover numerous applications to your selling game and personal life. Challenge trip to Europe questions that permeate your life. Pull the string. Know that the guts to fail causes success. Ask for turndowns. Purchase a plastic bucket. Shoot the ray gun. Stack the bricks. Avoid lofty platitudes. Create an army of non-negotiable factors. Make mystifying statements. Set up cliffhangers. Create theater-of-the-mind. Polish your star quality. Be honored with a testimonial dinner. And finally, always-always-always include The Fifth W.

That's the menu. For dessert, your greater success is the frosting on the cake. Will you accept a tangy, citrus flavor?

What are you thinking of?

Notes

Summary

The super salesperson knows he or she cannot simply march in place. Being unique and a top performer requires a constant striving for new weapons and a zest for the limelight. Herein lies a philosophy that encourages a person you choose to persuade to reach out for your product or service or point of view in the same way a kitten reaches out for a ball of yarn. This book contains a mountain of innovative sales tactics that will enrich your individuality, persuasion-ability, and personal powers.

Discover Pulling the String, The Fifth W, Guts to Fail, Ray Gun, Cliffhangers, Theater of the Mind, Yo-yo Effect, Non-negotiable Factors, Star Quality, FBI Interrogation School Questions, Mystifying Statements, Carrots, Stacking the Bricks, Trip to Europe Questions, and more.

This book goes beyond those 'whats' with the author's alter ego, Jimmy Dover, whose chameleon-like ability to match up with different termperaments, educational backgrounds, and personalities leaves them feeling good and disposed to buy, as he demonstrates the 'hows' in an amazing montage of diverse selling situations.

About the Author

John R. Downes covered the globe as advertising man, school supplies company president, management consultant, and sales trainer for clients including Manufacturers Hanover, First Pennsylvania Bank, Sears, TG&Y, Walgreens, Target, Safeway, and Peugeot. His other books: NonConfrontation Selling…The One-on-One Revolution" and the mystery novel, "A Few Deadly Friends." He resides in Spokane, Washington.

9 780595 140909